EDWARD BOND

Lear

With Commentary and Notes by
PATRICIA HERN

BLOOMSBURY

Bloomsbury Methuen Drama

An imprint of Bloomsbury Publishing Plc

50 Bedford Square
London
WC1B 3DP
UK

1385 Broadway
New York
NY 10018
USA

www.bloomsbury.com

Bloomsbury is a registered trade mark of Bloomsbury Publishing Plc

Lear first published in 1972 by Eyre Methuen
This edition first published in 1983 by Methuen London Ltd
Reissued with a new cover design 1994
Reissued with additional material and a new cover design 2006
Reprinted 2007, 2009, 2012, 2013

Lear and Author's Preface © Edward Bond 1972
Commentary and Notes © Methuen London Ltd 1983, 2006

British Library Cataloguing-in-Publication Data
A catalogue record for this book is available from the British Library.

ISBN: PB: 978-0-4135-1950-4

Library of Congress Cataloging-in-Publication Data
A catalog record for this book is available from the Library of Congress.

Printed and bound in Great Britain

*Special thanks are due to Edward Bond for his help and
encouragement in the preparation of this edition*

Contents

Production photographs appear on pp. iv, xxiii, lii, liv, lvi and 103–8. Those of the original 1971 Royal Court production are by John Haynes, those of the 1982 Royal Shakespeare Company production are by Donald Cooper.

Notes on this edition

Sources of quotations are given throughout the introductory material, and fuller references to books and articles will be found in the list of Further Reading. References to Bond's plays are to the standard editions published in the Methuen Modern Plays series.

The text of *Lear* printed here is identical to the Modern Plays edition, and the page numbering is the same.

Where quotations from Bond are unattributed or attributed to letters, these are letters written to the editor during the preparation of this edition.

Three dots with square brackets, thus [...], indicate an editorial omission.

Lear and Gravedigger's Boy (end of Act 3 Scene 3). Royal Court, 1971.

Edward Bond

1934 18 July. Bond was born in Holloway, a northern suburb of
London, to parents he has described as being 'lower
working-class. But not London working-class'. His father
was a farm worker, who came to London in search of
employment when no longer able to find work enough on
the land.

1940 He was evacuated from London to Cornwall, then sent to
his grandparents near Ely, in the Fens area of
Cambridgeshire.

1946 He was sent to Crouch End Secondary Modern School in
north London — that is, he was classified as non-academic,
unsuitable for a grammar school education.

1948 Bond went with a school party to see the actor-manager
Donald Wolfit in Shakespeare's *Macbeth* at the Bedford
Theatre in Camden, London. 'For the very first time in my
life, I met somebody who was actually talking about my
problems, about the life I'd been living, the political
society around me.' (Interview with editors of *Theatre
Quarterly*, Vol. II, no. 5, Jan-Mar 1972) Bond later
explained that this was because Shakespeare stated the
problems in such a way that they had to be considered
politically.

1949 Bond left school and began a series of short-term jobs in
factories and offices.

1953 He was called up for National Service and sent to Austria as
a clerk in the Allied Army of Occupation. While in the
army he began writing, a short story first. This period also
sharpened his political awareness: 'You find in the army
that the class structures are not glossed over. They're very
medieval. There was brazen brutality.' (*Theatre Quarterly*,
Vol. II, no. 5)

**1955
-57** Bond went to as many plays as possible in London, being
especially impressed by the work of Joan Littlewood at
Stratford East and by the opportunities offered to new
writers by the Royal Court Theatre, London.

1958 Bond submitted two plays to the Royal Court Theatre:
Klaxon in Atreus' Place and *The Fiery Tree*. He was invited
by Keith Johnstone, playreader for the Royal Court, to join
the Writers' Group run by William Gaskill. Among those
young writers in the group were John Arden (whose plays
Live Like Pigs, Serjeant Musgrave's Dance and *The Happy
Haven* were staged at the Royal Court between 1958 and
1960), Arnold Wesker (during this period the Royal Court
presented his *Chicken Soup with Barley, Roots,* and *I'm
Talking About Jerusalem*) and Ann Jellicoe (*The Sport of
My Mad Mother* in 1958, *The Knack* in 1962). In an essay
written to mark 25 years of The English Stage Company at
the Royal Court, Ann Jellicoe described the character of
the Writers' Group:

> We tried to explore the nature of theatre. Believing as we
> did in theatre depending on action and images rather
> than words, we hardly ever analysed or discussed what
> we were doing, or each other's plays, or theories of
> playwriting. Sometimes we improvised around a set
> theme, sometimes from a spontaneous idea. (*At the
> Royal Court* edited by Richard Findlater, Amber Lane
> Press, p. 65)

Bond became a playreader for the Royal Court. During this
period he wrote three short pieces: *The Golden Age* (1959),
I Don't Want to Be Nice for the Writers' Group (1959) and
The Outing (1960). These were not given public
performance.

1962 9 December. *The Pope's Wedding* was directed by Keith
Johnstone for one performance only, as one of a series of
low-budget, Sunday-night productions at the Royal Court.
The reviews were, on the whole, encouraging. George
Devine, artistic director of the Royal Court, commissioned
a new play from Bond.

1963 Bond delivered the script of *Saved*. William Gaskill, now
artistic director of the Royal Court Theatre, decided to
direct it himself. As Bond recalls:

> It was lying about at the Court for a year before Bill
> Gaskill was appointed Artistic Director. He found the
> play in a drawer on his first morning at the job and
> decided — that day — to produce it.

1965 *Saved* was submitted to the Lord Chamberlain's Office — at
that time the government authority for the licensing of
plays for public performance in Britain. Severe cuts were
demanded before a licence would be granted. Bond refused
to cut his play.

3 November. Gaskill presented *Saved* as a club performance
for the English Stage Society, hoping thus to by-pass the
Lord Chamberlain's censorship. Most reviews were
extremely hostile, concentrating on the scene in which a
baby is stoned to death.

1966 13 January. Bond's adaptation of the Jacobean play, *A
Chaste Maid in Cheapside*, staged at the Royal Court
directed by Gaskill.

February. The Royal Court Theatre was prosecuted for
presenting *Saved* without a licence, found guilty and
ordered to pay £50 legal costs, but not otherwise penalised.

February. Bond was offered a £1,000 bursary by the Arts
Council. He was then working on the screenplay for
Antonioni's film *Blow Up*.

1966 Bond worked on a number of film scripts, for example,
-69 *Walkabout* directed by Nicholas Roeg.

1967 18 April. Bond translated *Three Sisters* by Chekhov for
Gaskill's production at the Royal Court Theatre in April.
Gaskill's second commission for an original work from
Bond led to *Early Morning*, which was banned from *all*
public performance by the Lord Chamberlain's Office.

31 March. The *Saved* prosecution had made it clear that
Club performances were not acceptable to the Lord
Chamberlain; despite this *Early Morning* was presented as a
club performance, and again on 7 April as an open rehearsal
to which critics were invited, followed by a discussion on
censorship, in which Bond and Gaskill participated.

1968 May. *Saved* and *Early Morning* won the George Devine
Award. Bond was then working on *Narrow Road to the
Deep North* on commission from the Canon of Coventry
Cathedral, to coincide with a 'Peoples and Cities
Conference' at Coventry.

24 June. Helped by a £50 grant from ATV, *Narrow Road
to the Deep North* opened at the Belgrade Theatre,
Coventry, directed by Gaskill's assistant Jane Howell. This
play was joint winner of the John Whiting Award.

September. The new Theatres Act became law, taking

censorship powers away from the Lord Chamberlain's
Office.

1969   The Royal Court Theatre presented a season of Bond's plays:
7 February. *Saved.*

19 February. *Narrow Road to the Deep North.*

13 March. *Early Morning.*

September-October. The British Council helped fund a tour
of *Saved* and *Narrow Road to the Deep North* to Belgrade,
Venice, Prague, Lublin and Warsaw. *Saved* shared first prize
at the Belgrade BITEF Festival.

During this time Bond collaborated with Keith Hack, a
director, on a translation of Brecht's *Roundheads and
Peakheads* (not performed). This involved Bond's studying
Shakespeare's *Measure of Measure* in some detail, a play
dealing with the rival demands of law and order, on the one
hand, and justice, on the other. This theme was later
explored by Bond in *Lear.*

1970   22 March. *Black Mass* was performed at the Lyceum
Theatre, London, to support the Anti-Apartheid Movement;
it was part of *Sharpeville Sequence: A Scene, a Story, and
Three Poems.*

Bond was already beginning work on *Lear.*

1971   April. *Passion* was presented as part of the Campaign for
Nuclear Disarmament, at Alexandra Park Racecourse.

29 September. *Lear* opened at the Royal Court directed
by William Gaskill to shocked reviews from most critics.

1973   January. Bond directed a production of *Lear* in German at
the renowned Burgtheater, Vienna.

22 May. *The Sea* had its first performance at the Royal
Court Theatre. In an interview for *The Times*, 22.5.73,
Bond described his intentions: 'I deliberately set out to
make an audience laugh. [. . .] I wanted deliberately to say
to an audience, "You mustn't despair. You mustn't be
afraid." ' Again, the play was directed by Gaskill.

October. *Lear* was a prize-winner at the BITEF Festival.

14 November. *Bingo* was directed by Jane Howell at the
Northcott Theatre, Exeter. The play is sub-titled *Scenes of
Money and Death* and offers an austere image of
Shakespeare's last years.

1974   24 March. Bond's translation of Wedekind's *Spring
Awakening* was performed by the National Theatre
Company at the Old Vic Theatre, London. Bond also

worked on an adaptation of Ibsen's *The Master Builder* for
an American televisión company, but it was not produced.

1975   18 November. *The Fool*, exploring the life of the nineteenth-
century poet John Clare, was given its first performance at
the Royal Court Theatre, directed by Peter Gill.

1976   8 June. *Stone*, commissioned by the Gay Sweatshop
Theatre, was staged at the Institute of Contemporary Arts
in London.
12 July. *We Come to the River* opened at the Royal Opera
House, Covent Garden in London, libretto by Bond and
music by Hans Werner Henze.
12 July. Bond's adaptation of *The White Devil* by the
Jacobean playwright John Webster was first performed by
the National Theatre Company at the Old Vic.
25 October/22 November. *Grandma Faust* and *The Swing*
performed at Ed Berman's Almost Free Theatre, London,
directed by Jack Emery. Together the plays form the
double-bill *A-A-America!*
29-30 November. Bond read a selection of his translations
of Brecht pieces for the Tyneside Theatre Company in
Newcastle.
The Fool was nominated in *Plays and Players* as the Best
Play of 1976, winning the London Critics Award.

1977   May. Bond received an Honorary Doctorate from the
University of Yale.
October. He took up a Northern Arts Literary Fellowship,
working at the Universities of Durham and Newcastle.

1978   13 January. *The Bundle* had its premiere at the Warehouse,
the Royal Shakespeare Company's studio theatre in London,
directed by Howard Davies.
15 February. Bond read a selection of his translations of
work by Brecht at the Roundhouse, London.
June. Bond began rehearsing his production of his new
play, *The Woman*, at the new National Theatre on London's
South Bank.
August. *The Woman* was the first new play to be performed
in the Olivier, the largest auditorium at the National Theatre.
Bond's reshaping and re-interpretation of the events sur-
rounding the Fall of Troy was greeted by some critical
scorn, but generally the play aroused serious interest.

1979   8 March. *The Worlds* was first performed by the Newcastle
University Theatre Society at the Newcastle Playhouse.

21 November. *The Worlds* was performed by the Activists Youth Theatre Club at the Royal Court Theatre Upstairs. Bond wrote a series of essays, poems, stories and statements while he was directing this production; these were published, with the play, under the title *The Activists Papers*.

1981   21 July. *Restoration*, directed by Bond, opened at the Royal Court Theatre. The play is set in eighteenth-century England and uses songs to comment on the action.

1982   Bond published *The Cat*, described as 'A Story for Music'.

1982   January. Bond directed his play, *Summer*, at the National Theatre, London. It shows a meeting between two women whose lives were previously linked during the German occupation of their seaside region of Eastern Europe.

1982   July. The Royal Shakespeare Company presented *Lear* at The Other Place, their studio theatre in Stratford-upon-Avon, directed by Barry Kyle. This production was part of the same season as a new production of Shakespeare's *King Lear* in the larger theatre. As at *Lear's* premiere in 1971, the critics shared two dominant responses: they drew comparisons between Bond's play and Shakespeare's, and they expressed shock, or at least concern, about the violence represented on stage.

> Mr Bond has not merely given the Lear story a modern context, he has repointed the entire edifice. [. . .] Mr Bond's potent theatrical imagery and a fine production stumble into a muddled political allegory, but it is one with great visceral force beneath its arguments. (*The Times* 1.7.82)

In the five years following the premiere production of *Lear* in 1971, the play was produced in eleven other countries: Holland (Amsterdam, 1971); West Germany (Frankfurt, Trier, Bonn, 1972; Munich, Ulm, Nuremberg, Berlin, 1973); Austria (Vienna, Linz, 1973); U.S.A. (New Haven, 1973); New Zealand (Auckland, 1973); Australia (Sydney, 1974); Denmark (radio, Aarhus, 1975); Switzerland (Geneva, 1975); France (Lyons, 1975); Yugoslavia (Sarajevo, 1975); Italy (L'Aquila, 1976); but only once more in Britain: Liverpool, 1975. (Information from Hay and Roberts. *Bond: A Companion*)

Epic/Rational theatre

Epic isn't a style but a philosophical undertaking. It emphasises the origin of morality and reason in human work and creativity: that the concepts of absurdity and nihilism are not applicable to human affairs, except as a form of decadence; that art is not universal, not some ideal statement that appeals to all people, but is class-derived and historical; that art is, in fact, the creation of value by incorporating the structures in human, historical development into human images and into new, enriched, more rational forms of consciousness. (Letter to his publisher, 9 February, 1982)

The forms of the new drama will be epic. [. . .] An epic play tells a story and says why it happened. This gives it a beginning, a middle and an end joined together in a truthful way. [. . .] Theatre must talk of the causes of human misery and the sources of human strength. ('A Note to Young Writers', *The Worlds*, pp. 107-109)

Culture will be each individual's understanding of his community and his commitment to it. [. . .] The artist's job is to make the process public, to create public images, literal or figurative, in signs, sound and movement, of the human condition — public images in which our species recognizes itself and confirms its identity. (Introduction to *The Fool*, pp. xiv-vi)

These statements focus attention on three related aspects of Bond's work. First, there is his emphatic commitment to an ideology, or rather to something wider, less merely intellectual, a rationale for living, a morality made practical. Then there is his translation of that commitment into a dramatic form which can reflect and affirm his argument through its structure, gestures and language. Finally there is the audience's response to the presented play, a movement from angry recognition of the injustices and irrationalities still brutalising society, towards a belief in man's ability painfully to push aside the dead weight of a decadent system and live rationally, with dignity and humanity, in a socialist

world. Idea, expression, reaction: the pattern is didactic. Bond
requires the theatre to teach truths which he feels cannot be taugl
through the traditional institutions of state, school and church,
since these are crippled and corrupted by capitalism and the
bourgeoisie, defenders of the status quo.

> Society resists change. It's based on laws and property relations
> that benefit the rulers of the old social order. They run it on the
> old form of consciousness calcified in universities, churches,
> theatres, customs, opinions, and so on . . . ('On Weapons', *The
> Worlds*, p. 114)

Bond here uses 'society' to mean the Establishment, the social
order, rather than the masses of people living within it. The theatre
— even though it at present operates largely within a system of
state subsidy and commercial enterprise and so might therefore be
suspect — can offer a platform for protest. It can vividly reinterpret
the political and economic processes underlying our history, our
traditions, our culture and our life-style. Art, especially the theatre,
in other words, is not to be seen as an ornamental and essentially
frivolous retreat from the soul-destroying business of living, nor as
an elaborate, self-justifying distraction for aesthetes and
intellectuals, nor as a complacent celebration of contemporary
civilisation. In a programme note for *We Come to the River*, Bond
stressed again the rationale behind all art, the basis for its claim to
significance:

> Men without politics would be animals, and art without politics
> would be trivial. [. . .] Art is the most public of activities. [. . .]
> Art is the expression of the conviction that we can have a
> rational relationship with the world and each other. It isn't the
> faith or hope that we can, it is the *demonstration* that we can.
> [. . .] Art is always optimistic and rational — in this way: it
> makes the present relationship between people easier to
> understand, by destroying cloaks of sentimentality, hypocrisy
> and myth, and it makes the potential rationality of these
> relationships more certain. It does this partly through its choice
> of subject — but the important thing is the integrity of its
> objectivity.

Two ideas recur: one is rationality; the other is each man's need to
understand his relationship with the society he inhabits. Bond
demands that the individual should not only recognise how that
society has been shaped by political movements in history but

should also appreciate that the process is continuous. Society is constantly being changed by technological innovations, economic forces, movements of population from the land to the city or from one country to another, and shifts in the balance of political power. The danger Bond sees in this relationship between a man's idea of himself, of what he can and should require of life, and the prevailing technology and social organisation is that the ordinary individual does not own and therefore does not control that technology and those social forms. So he is forced to cramp and distort his natural and reasonable needs to fit an unnatural, irrational model. And when he can no longer endure such a crippling constriction, he may become violent in his anger.

Rationality, Bond argues, means socialism as opposed to capitalism or fascism. Capitalism and fascism are irrational in that they violate men's inherent right to freedom, to dignity, and to the pursuit of a happiness or a fulfilment that does not imply the subjection or subversion of others. All these being evidently reasonable expectations, any encroachment on them is demonstrably *un*reasonable. The rational is threatened by the irrational through unjust class divisions, the inequitable distribution of wealth, privilege and power, and the application of law and order − seen as a travesty of justice − to preserve the status quo.

'Morality' in this context becomes a euphemism for the bourgeois-capitalist ethic. It requires those without privilege and power to endure and conform in the *belief* that it is blesséd to be meek, and the *hope* that one distant day somewhere over the rainbow the down-trodden poor will inherit the earth − provided that they do not blot their copy-book first by disruptive behaviour in the here-and-now. Yet, Bond explains, it is impossible − irrational − to expect people to endure such violations of their rights and needs without becoming de-humanized and full of despair.

> If the social environment isn't one that helps us live humanly (socialism) but helps in our exploitation (capitalism) or makes us beasts or machines (fascism) then our emotions tend to deteriorate into fear, tension and racial and religious paranoia which leads to aggression, vandalism, child battering and other forms of violence. (*The Worlds*, p. 89)

This is the process demonstrated in *Saved* when five young men, bored and disaffected, with little to give purpose or fulfilment to their lives, begin to play cruel games with a baby in a pram. There is generated a growing excitement which culminates in the baby's violent death. The baby's mother has doped it with aspirin to silence its demands on her time and affections, so now it cannot communicate its terror or its pain. The lads' first instincts — 'Little bleeder's 'alf dead a fright.' 'Mind yer don't 'urt it' — are overtaken by the heightened excitement of a forbidden sport.

> PETE (*quietly*). Yer can do what yer like.
> BARRY. Might as well enjoy ourselves.
> PETE (*quietly*). Yer don't get a chance like this everyday.
>
> FRED *throws the stone*. (*Saved*, p. 69)

This episode sparked off vehement protest when the play was first performed. There was, for example, J.W. Lambert's review in the *Sunday Times*, 7 November, 1965:

> **Past the limits of brutality**
> Cruelty and viciousness, on the stage, are no strangers to the theatre. But was there ever a psychopathic exercise so lovingly dwelt on as this, spun out with such apparent relish and refinement of detail? [. . .] Things as horrible as this baby-killing, and worse, happen everyday; but it is not enough merely to enact them. Without the shaping hand of art in the writing the result is only reporting. And when to reporting is added the intensification of stagecraft and powerful acting, and the prolongation of sadistic antics far beyond the time needed to make a valid point, in circumstances carelessly rigged, the conclusion is inescapable: that we are being offered not a keenly understanding, and therefore implicitly compassionate, study of deprived and unfortunate people, but a concocted opportunity for vicarious beastliness — still, I naively suppose, a minority taste.

There are important assumptions behind such a response, and they still colour critical assessment of this and much of Bond's work, despite his energetic defence of his aims and methods. There is, most significantly, the concession that cruelty and violence are familiar and generally acceptable elements in drama, but only so long as *the shaping hand of art* has conspicuously transformed these horrible things that happen every day into aesthetically pleasing dramatic devices. The audience can then appreciate *the understanding and compassionate study of deprived and unfortunate people* without being made uncomfortable, without feeling savage anger or passionate distress and the need to do something to prevent such horror being an every day event in our society. Cruelty and violence become merely points of literary discussion.

Bond in contrast demands that the theatre must attack what he sees as bourgeois sensibilities, resting on a sentimental complacency. He intends to jolt the audience into active awareness. The theatre is for him a political activity. Another assumption behind J.W. Lambert's review is that Bond is 'only reporting', that the play is 'carelessly rigged'. This shows no appreciation of Bond's very deliberate development of a highly organised form – his epic theatre.

Epic: for many people this term is associated with at least three literary landmarks. The concept was defined by Aristolte in his *Poetics;* there he distinguished between the action of tragedy, which operated most effectively within concentrated but significant segments of time and space (the classical Unities), and the more extended action of the epic which encompassed the history of a nation. The epic

> related a great and complete action which attaches itself to the fortunes of a people, or to the destiny of mankind, and sums up the life of a period. The story and deeds of those who pass across its wide canvas are linked with the larger movement of which the men themselves are but a part. (S.H. Butcher, *Aristotle's Theory of Poetry and Fine Art*)

The epics of Homer and Virgil describe the exploits of a hero, or fellowship of heroes. The *Odyssey* and the *Aeneid,* for instance, celebrate the emergence of a nation, or rather of a nation's conception of its past history. The structure is episodic; the hero moves through a sequence of experiences, each one complete as a short narrative, yet the whole is given unity by the continuity of the central figure, and significance by the clearly stated objective behind the hero's journey.

This panoramic celebration of a nation's traditions, a blend of history and folklore, is also a feature of the Shakespearean epic. In the *Revels History of Drama in English,* Shakespeare's four major

history plays — *Richard II, Henry IV* Parts 1 and 2, and *Henry V*
— are referred to as the *Henriad:*

> ... they do have a remarkable coherence and they possess that
> quality which in our time we take to be the chief characteristic
> of epic: large scale, heroic action, involving many men and
> many activities, tracing the movement of a nation or people
> through violent change from one condition to another. (Volume
> III, p. 270)

An understanding of what it is to be English (from Shakespeare's
historical viewpoint) is presented dramatically through the rise and
fall of powerful men, figures rooted in a known past and whose
actions and fate are, therefore, already established. The interest,
then, is less in what happens, than in how and why it happens.
Since the action must move through decades, rather than
concentrate on one moment of conflict, and extend across the
wide political map of Renaissance Europe, it follows that the
structure of Shakespearean epics, like the classical, is episodic.
Each event — a key battle, a conspiracy, the death of a king — is a
dramatised story in itself, yet is always felt to be part of a greater
movement.

'Epic' is also the term used by the German dramatist and poet,
Bertolt Brecht (1898-1956), to describe his kind of drama. The
extracts quoted here are taken from *Brecht on Theatre*, translated
by John Willett, London, Methuen, 1964.

> It is understood that the *radical transformation of the theatre*
> can't be the result of some artistic whim. It has simply to
> conform to the whole radical transformation of the mentality
> of our time. [. . .] The essential point of the epic theatre is
> perhaps that it appeals less to the feelings than to the spectator's
> reason (p. 23).

> Human behaviour is shown as alterable; man himself as
> dependent on certain political factors and at the same time as
> capable of altering them (p. 86).

> It [epic theatre] by no means renounces emotion, least of all
> the sense of justice, the urge to freedom, and righteous anger
> (p. 227).

> The bourgeois theatre's performances always aim at smoothing
> over contradictions, at creating false harmony, at idealization.

Conditions are reported as if they could not be otherwise (p. 277).

As well as proclaiming the consciously political and reforming purpose of his epic theatre, Brecht drew up a scheme to illustrate the significant differences in form and style between his epic drama and the old, traditionally 'dramatic' theatre cherished by the bourgeoisie. These are a few of the points made (p. 37):

DRAMATIC	EPIC
plot	narrative
implicates the spectator in a stage situation	turns the spectator into an observer but
wears down his capacity for action	arouses his capacity for action
provides him with sensations	forces him to take decisions
the human being is taken for granted	the human being is the object of inquiry
he is unalterable	he is alterable and able to alter
thought determines being	social being determines thought

One crucial difference between the earlier forms of epic and the Brechtian epic is that the former generally endorsed society's or the nation's sense of its principles and practices, whereas Brecht intended to challenge those assumptions in his own time, reinterpreting stories from the past where they seemed useful to illuminate the present (for example, he 'reinterpreted' Marlowe's *Edward II* and Shakespear's *Coriolanus*). Clearly Bond's intentions are closer to the spirit of Brecht than of Homer or Virgil or even Shakespeare. However, Bond himself stressed an important distinction between his theatre and that of Brecht: 'Brecht wrote in the time of the "masses". I write in the time of the "individuals" — yet this must be seen not as a reactionary retreat but as a further concretization of socialism' (Letter, 4 March 1982). In other words, Bond demonstrates political movements through the experience of a handful of distinct and separate characters caught up in a historical process.

Bond's statement that an epic play tells a story and says why it happened points to the predominance of action over character, even while he is concerned to present his selected individuals vividly and with conviction. A story is a linked sequence of events and can involve elements other than human motivation — elements such as natural disasters, the intervention of super-human forces, the effects of chance or coincidence — but there is generally a progression through successive incidents towards some kind of climax which makes sense of what has gone before. A good story can establish its own rules and logic but it must then stick to them or wreck its created world. Some of the stories in Bond's plays are small in scale, following a few apparently unimportant people through the dispiriting routines imposed on them by an irrational society but given a sharp focus by the sudden eruption of violence (as in *The Pope's Wedding* and *Saved*). Some of his stories are set in a distant land, in an uncertain time, and have the clear outlines and 'once-upon-a-time-ness' of fables or folklore made vehemently political (as in *Narrow Road to the Deep North* and *The Bundle*). Others of his stories take princes and generals through the landscapes of classical and Shakespearean epics (as in *The Woman* and *Lear*). In each case, Bond is concerned, as he explains in his 'Notes on Acting *The Woman*', to 'analyse these events, not merely reproduce them' (*The Woman*, p. 127). Through the selection and relating of events he intends to reveal the historical, political and social forces controlling people's lives.

The plays are a series of episodes, each dealing with one or two incidents in a deliberately uncluttered manner. Bond presents only what is immediately relevant to the political situation being described. For example, a woman is pregnant, married to a gravedigger's son; she is anxious about the presence in her home of a political fugitive; she is a victim of a brutal attack by the soldiers of the ruling military regime; she becomes a revolutionary; then, in her turn, she assumes power at the head of a strong-arm military junta. The outline is stark. Bond does not dwell on the details of accumulated experience and the subjective life which make this woman unique; he concentrates on *what happens to her* and shows what she then becomes as a factor in a political equation. He tells her story and says why it happened. The audience looks at her, briefly, in a staccato sequence of significant moments; it is not invited to *share* her experience, but to *recognise* it, moment by moment, as the product of changing historical and political realities. The point about historical forces, after all, is that they affect people and so do not remain merely abstractions.

Bond may not allow his characters to reveal (or, as he would say, to construct) and contemplate their inner life as explicitly as, for example, Shakespeare allows Hamlet to do through extended soliloquy. But he is nonetheless concerned to represent his characters' individual experience dramatically, to imply an emotional life and a consistent inner logic through their responses to the changing conditions of their world. Their actions, the features of the epic story, must spring convincingly out of these implied feelings. It is the sense of a character's continuing inner life that enables the audience to understand the connections between episodic events. The theatrical silence separating the Cordelia who stands helplessly with her face covered by her hands beside the body of her husband (p. 30) from the incisively ruthless guerilla leader on the battlefield (pp. 42-45) must not be empty, or else the two events will have no sensible connection apart from the whim of the story-teller. Bond's argument depends upon the audience's understanding of and acceptance of Cordelia's capacity for suffering, anger and calculated retaliation. His conviction that every response is political (in that every response is governed by the individual's relationship to his society) springs from a dramatically powerful conception of the continuous interaction of thought and feeling, reason and emotion, of the outside world and the individual's inner life.

> I regard subjective experience as very important: but often I have to create that subjective-presence on stage very swiftly and without demonstrating the process of inner-invention. [. . .] What is needed now is a clearer understanding of our relationship to the world via the means of culture and society: that our subjectivity isn't something that differentiates us from our objective society but does in fact the opposite, makes us a part of (not merely something in) our society. And that it's only by making society (as the relationships between people) rational that the individual can gain his or her personal freedom. [. . .] Finally, is it clear that I am not interested in the old dichotomy between reason and emotion? I mean the rational psyche to be fully emotional. It's its relationship to the world which is rational. It doesn't mean that subjectivity is emptied of emotion. It means that emotions are, in fact, more pronounced and full. It also allows for the emotions associated with tragedy and waste and suffering. (Letter, 4 March 1982)

Thus it would be wrong to think of Bond's epic theatre as no more than a political manifesto, couched in dialogue form but still remaining on the level of stated doctrine rather than drama. Not only is Bond concerned to dramatise the emotions and motivations of his characters, he is also emphatic about the importance of what he calls the 'texture' of characters; that is, the imaginative selection of details which combine to create a vivid, convincing and provocative individual with the appearance of solidity, of reality. It is essential, if Bond's theatre is to be effective, that he create worlds in his plays that are full of vitality and seem *true*. The inside of Alen's shack in *The Pope's Wedding* is full of solid not merely symbolic piles of newspapers and canned foods; it is a real chair that Len settles down to mend at the end of *Saved*; in *Narrow Road to the Deep North* the pot which a young monk gets stuck on his head may represent a whole religious tradition but it also is in danger of suffocating poor Kiro since it is palpably 'real', has weight, can shut out the air.

In 'Types of Drama', one section of *The Activists Papers*, Bond explains what the ideal relationship would be between the ideas contained within the plays and the 'texture' of the plays enacted in the theatre (*The Worlds*, pp. 129-131):

> Incidents would be chosen to show how historical problems arise and how they lead to resolutions. Movements spread over long periods and involving masses of people might be reflected in stories, often in simple stories. The characters wouldn't be moved by personal motives but by forms of history. [. . .] Indeed we'd show the power of historical forces by showing the individual ordinariness and human vulnerability and strength of the characters who live in it. [. . .] In it [epic pattern] there's no conceptual division between descriptions of a battle or a meal, between a battlefield or a dinner plate — no bewilderment, no creative no-man's land. [. . .] Each guarantees the existence of the other, each makes the other real. The family at table, the soldiers in the field, the refugees, the children playing, all human actions, human objects and the human mind may be completely shown in the arc of one story.

Bond's presence as the story-teller is always felt, even in the theatre — this is one feature of the objectivity of his epic form referred to in the programme note for *We Come to the River*. It is the 'objectivity' of the observer-narrator who tells his audience how the world *is*, what he *sees*, not what he *uniquely* feels or imagines (a subjective vision) but what he knows to be *generally* true.

Plot

Act I

Act One consists of seven scenes. It begins with Lear's visit to the
great defensive wall he is having built to ensure, he claims, the
peace and security of his people against his enemies, the Dukes of
Cornwall and North. His party includes his two daughters, Bodice
and Fontanelle, his adviser Warrington, and an old councillor.
Despite the protests of his daughters, he executes a man for causing
the death of another worker on the wall. Bodice and Fontanelle
grasp this opportunity to announce their intention to marry
Cornwall and North and to destroy Lear's wall. Civil war follows.
Warrington is captured by the sisters − each of whom has tried
unsuccessfully to suborn him into betraying Lear, assassinating the
dukes and becoming consort of the victorious and newly widowed
princess. The sisters have him mutilated, then released. He is deaf
and dumb, but not blind. Lear becomes a fugitive and is given
shelter out of pity by a gravedigger's son despite the anxiety of the
young man's pregnant wife. Warrington tries to kill Lear, but
merely wounds him before running away. Soldiers from Bodice and
Fontanelle arrive, shoot the gravedigger's son and rape his wife.
Lear is taken captive. A carpenter from the nearby village, in love
with the Boy's wife (who, it is then revealed, is called Cordelia),
kills the soldiers in retribution for their actions.

Act II

Act Two also consists of seven short scenes. The dukes hope to
save Lear's life, but they do not prevent Lear from being brought
for trial before a judge who has been ordered by Bodice to
aggravate and then condemn Lear. Lear does not recognise his
daughters. He is appalled by his own mirror reflection which seems
to him to be the image of a caged beast for which he feels intense
pity. Fontanelle is increasingly distracted from politics by her
lovers, while Bodice plots to take over supreme power and get rid
of her sister. The dukes flee, but are recaptured. Lear is visited in
prison by the ghost of the gravedigger's boy and by the ghosts of
Bodice and Fontanelle as young girls. A revolutionary army, led by

Cordelia and the carpenter, overthrows the sisters' regime.
Fontanelle and Bodice are both captured. Fontanelle is shot and
her body is cut open while Lear watches, fascinated by the neatness
and beauty of the anatomy and shocked to learn that this is the
body of his daughter, whom he had come to regard as a monster.
Bodice fights for life, but is also killed. The carpenter recognises
Lear as a potential danger, but Cordelia will not allow his
execution. Instead Lear is blinded and then set free to wander with
the ghost of the gravedigger's boy. Cordelia orders resumption of
work on Lear's wall, which means that the peasants' land and
livelihood are taken from them and the people are forced to labour
on the wall. Lear feels that he must warn Cordelia of the dangers of
such a policy. He is now acutely sensitive to the suffering around
him.

Act III

Act Three has four scenes. Some months have passed and Lear has
come to terms with his blindness. He is living at the boy's house
with Thomas and Susan, a young couple. Susan is pregnant. She is
loved by a man from the village, John, but refuses to leave Thomas
for him. Lear has become a focus for opposition to Cordelia's
regime. People gather to hear the political parables he tells. Two
deserters from the wall arrive: one is a petty criminal who used to
trade illegally in tobacco and other goods; the other is Ben, a
young orderly who brought food to Lear in prison. Cordelia's
soldiers come in search of the deserters but leave without
discovering them, warning Lear that he will in future be under
surveillance. The old councillor, who has successfully switched
allegiance with every shift of power, informs Lear that he is now
under house arrest. Ben and the other deserter are arrested. Ben is
happy to return to the wall, to organise opposition there to
Cordelia's government. The other deserter is to be hanged. Lear is
angered by the cruelty and hypocrisy of the new regime and
despairs of his ability to change things. The boy's ghost, pale and
emaciated, tries to persuade Lear to give up the struggle and live
in quiet seclusion. Cordelia comes, with the carpenter, to convince
Lear that he must stop opposing her. Lear says that he cannot be
silent and tries to teach her the necessity for pity, but she argues
that hardness is needed to make a leader strong enough to build a
better world. She warns Lear that he will be tried and sentenced to
death. The boy's ghost follows her, distressed that she is unaware
of his presence. Lear tells Thomas and Susan that he must make a

journey with Susan's help. The boy's ghost stumbles in, bleeding —
he has been attacked by pigs and must die a second time, leaving
Lear free to go to the wall and show in action what he has learnt
about the mistakes he made as king. Taking a spade Lear climbs the
wall and begins to shovel earth down from the top, continuing even
when challenged by an officer in Cordelia's army. Lear is shot. The
officer hustles the few bystanders away so that only the wall and
Lear's body remain.

Left to right: Old Councillor, Lear, Fontanelle, Cornwall, Bodice,
North. (Act 2 Scene 1). Royal Court, 1971.

Commentary

Structure

> I know exactly what I'm going to say. I know exactly the order
> of the scenes and what's going to happen in them, and what
> character has to be there at what point. The difficulty is to get
> them there — that's the painful thing. I sort of work out a
> diagram. ('Drama and the Dialectics of Violence', interview,
> *Theatre Quarterly*, Vol. II No. 5, Jan.-March 1972, p. 12)

Bond's account of his approach to the organisation of action and
relationships in the play draws attention to the painstaking
management of material required by an epic subject. The structure
of *Lear* has affinities both with the sequences of plays written by a
classical Greek dramatist such as Aeschylus and with Shakespeare's
historical epics. The three-act form can be seen to work in a
manner similar to the *Orestia* of Aeschylus: the first play of that
trilogy shows Queen Clytemnestra successfully destroying her
husband, Agamemnon, and assuming power with her lover,
Aegisthus; however, her young son Orestes is smuggled away to
become the future instrument of retribution. The central play
shows Clytemnestra's regime apparently well established; Orestes
returns to avenge his father's murder by killing his mother, but
then he in his turn is pursued by the Furies as punishment for his
action, even though his motives were honourable. The final play
shows a resolution of the rival claims of vengeance and retribution
through the evolution of a new concept of enlightened justice.
Each play can stand on its own, yet each gains its full significance
from being seen as part of a developing idea. It is the pattern of
dialectic, progressing from the thesis (the dominant idea of the first
play or act), through the antithesis (an alternative or conflicting
idea), to the synthesis of the final part. And it is the pattern
described by Bond in his Preface to *Lear*:

> Act One shows a world dominated by myth. Act Two shows the
> clash between myth and reality, between superstitious men and
> the autonomous world. Act Three shows a resolution of this, in
> the world we prove real by dying in it.

This stresses the thematic importance of the three-act structure which gives coherence and point to the eighteen short scenes making up the play.

That each act follows the arc of a dominant idea is reflected in the rhythms of the plot: each act moves from a point or phase of conflict to some kind of resolution. Act One presents Lear at a moment of crisis: the autocrat challenged and deposed. Then the wheel turns with his fall and capture (he will face punishment for his earlier abuses of power), bringing his daughters to the top but also elevating a new Nemesis to pursue the prosecutors of the old king. Cordelia and the carpenter are established as future instruments of retribution. Act Two presents Bodice and Fontanelle at the height of their power and their tyranny, with Bodice especially caught up in the conflict between her self-image and the political reality as well as in the conflict with Cordelia's revolutionaries. By the end of the act, the sisters have been killed and Lear has — like another Greek tragic hero, Oedipus — been blinded for being the product of an irrational and inhumane system of privilege, a myth of kingship; yet he is also given a new freedom to discover the truth about his responsibilities towards the society he inhabits, to become aware where once he was morally blind. Act Three begins with Lear enjoying a kind of serenity and status as a John the Baptist-cum-Christ figure, talking to the people in parables. But here, too, there is conflict: between Lear's personal prestige and well-being on the one hand, and an insistent need for some positive political action on the other. His role as guru to the masses is an evasion of his real responsibility; he is no longer brutal but his preaching in a pastoral retreat, with paternalistic arrogance, does nothing to change the realities of Cordelia's totalitarian rule. The confrontation with Cordelia leads to Lear's final action, an attempt to throw down the wall that he and, after him, Cordelia had used to imprison the people. Thomas and Susan are left to build a better world from their understanding of the rationale behind Lear's assault on the wall. Each act contains the information needed to explain its situations and significance, to make the events seem coherent, and each one builds to a recognisable climax, yet there is an important relationship between them — that relationship described by Bond in his Preface to the play.

The thematic clarity of the three-act structure does not, however, invalidate Bond's decision to present the play's action through a series of short scenes. It is this episodic structure that links *Lear* to the Shakespearean epics, each episode dramatising

one significant moment in the shifting balance of political power
which makes up a nation's evolution. The action covers a
considerable span of time and moves abruptly from one location to
the next. The audience is able to view two or three lines of activity,
switching quickly from one to another, and thus to gain a god's-eye
view of the historical processes which have shaped society. In the
Theatre Quarterly interview, Bond spoke of the reasons behind his
use of this epic form:

> I felt it was important not only to know what was happening in
> the room I might be in, but also what was happening in that
> room over there, that house down the road. So that in order to
> say something useful about experience now, one has to keep
> track of all these things. The play keeps an eye on what's going
> on, you know — I think that's what my structure does. (p. 11)

From King Lear to Lear

> We have to correct the false views on which our culture is
> founded. [. . .] A false culture sustains itself by a false idea of
> human nature. [. . .] Our own culture is based on the idea that
> people are naturally violent. It is used to justify the violence and
> authoritarianism that saturate our state, although in fact it is the
> state that provokes violence and authoritarianism. [. . .] But the
> social moral of Shakespeare's *Lear* is this: endure till in time the
> world will be made right. That's a dangerous moral for us. We
> have less time than Shakespeare. ('*Lear*: Saving Our Necks' from
> the programme of the Liverpool Everyman Theatre's production
> of *Lear*, October 1975)

> Shakespeare says that Lear's suffering and partial, ineffective
> illumination represent the fallible condition of all human
> goodness. The problem is seen to be political but the solution
> given isn't — it recommends calmness and acceptance. ('Types
> of Drama', *The Worlds*, p. 126)

> As Shakespeare himself knew, the peace, the reconciliation that
> he created on the stage would not last an hour on the street.
> (Introduction, *Plays Two*, p. x)

These statements suggest why Bond felt particularly challenged by
Shakespeare's *King Lear* and what his re-creation of that story was
intended to achieve. The political problem in Shakespeare's play has
to do with power and responsibility: a privileged elite holds power
and wealth, making decisions which are shown to be unreasonable

in human terms as well as irresponsible politically. Instead of
following King Lear's progress towards self-knowledge and
reconciliation, the play can be seen as tracing historical movements
in an epic way. For example, in his essay 'Lear as King', David Pirie
draws attention to aspects of Shakespeare's drama which seem to
have affinities with Bond's approach.

> But the play explores more than the mental agony of Lear as a
> man. It also documents the physical torment to which, as
> abdicating king, he exposes his subjects. [. . .] Lear does
> admittedly discover — however belatedly for a head of state —
> that society is cruelly unfair to the poor, and that the
> dispensation of justice by a fallible human being is exceedingly
> difficult. But he remains incapable of relating these insights
> either to his own responsibilities as king or to the immediate
> situation. (*Critical Quarterly* Vol. 22, No. 2, Summer 1980,
> pp. 10-11)

The novelist and essayist George Orwell (1903-50), in his essay
'Lear, Tolstoy and The Fool', acknowledged the political nature of
the action of Shakespeare's *King Lear*, but saw it as one aspect
only of an all-informing idea of renunciation implicit in the two
moods of the play:

> One is the mood of disgust in which Lear repents, as it were, for
> having been a king, and grasps for the first time the rottenness
> of formal justice and vulgar morality. The other is the mood of
> impotent fury in which he wreaks imaginary revenges upon
> those who have wronged him. [. . .] Only at the end does he
> realise, as a sane man, that power, revenge and victory are not
> worthwhile. (*Shooting an Elephant and Other Essays*, Secker
> and Warburg, 1950, p. 46)

For Bond such an abdication of political responsibility is
unacceptable, unreasonable, a sign of moral collapse rather than a
return to sanity. His Lear is offered just such a retreat from
political activity by the ghost of the Gravedigger's Boy in Act III
scene ii:

> Send these people away. Let them learn to bear their own
> sufferings. [. . .] There's a spring hidden in the wood. I'll take
> you there every day to drink. Lie down. Look how tired you
> are. Lie down. (pp. 80-81)

Briefly Lear succumbs, but he soon realises that it is such selfish

quietness that must be renounced, not active involvement in the
world:

> I've suffered so much, I made all the mistakes in the world and I
> pay for each of them. I cannot be forgotten. I am in their
> minds. (p. 84)

Bond argues that by a theatrically effective sleight of hand in *King
Lear* Shakespeare has transmuted the political problem into a
personal conflict, so that, while the individual offenders are
punished and justice of some kind appears to have been done, the
system itself survives. For Shakespeare Lear's frailties and his
failures do not preclude the possibility of his reinstatement as king.

> ALBANY. . . . For us, we will resign,
>   During the life of this Old Majesty,
>   To him our absolute power. (V iii, 297-299)

Bond could accept neither a return to the bad old ways nor the
despondent resignation expressed in Edgar's final speech:

> The weight of this sad time we must obey;
> Speak what we feel, not what we ought to say.
> The oldest hath borne most: we that are young
> Shall never see so much, nor live so long. (V iii, 322-325)

Bond's work is bleak in many respects but, as he explained in the
Liverpool Everyman Theatre's programme for *Lear*, it is essential
to its political effectiveness that the play offer a way out of the
society dominated by fear and violence. The death of Bond's Lear
looks backwards to the mistakes he must expiate but also forwards
to the possibility of a more rational society that may be shaped by
succeeding generations' understanding of the event.

> My Lear makes a gesture in which he accepts responsibility for
> his life and commits himself to action. [. . .] My Lear's gesture
> mustn't be seen as final. That would make the play a part of the
> theatre of the absurd and that, like perverted science, is a
> reflection of no-culture. The human condition isn't absurd; it's
> only our society which is absurd. Lear is very old and has to die
> anyway. He makes his gesture only to those who are learning
> how to live.

Bond's certainties are significant: his Lear's gesture *mustn't be seen*
as final. Shakespeare's intentions lie buried in the language of his
play but Bond is anxious to explain his purposes and processes, to

avoid ambiguities and escape the symbolic or purely aesthetic speculations of critics and academics. He has provided his own commentary on structure and meaning.

Bond's choice of Lear as a subject inevitably creates certain expectations in his audience. It is 'known' that his story concerns the surrender of power to daughters who prove ungrateful and unscrupulous but who are ultimately punished for their inhumanity. Shakespeare gives his Lear three daughters — Regan, Goneril and Cordelia. Bond's Lear has only two daughters — Bodice and Fontanelle. There are parallels between Regan and Bodice and between Goneril and Fontanelle, quite apart from the rhythmical echoes within the pairs of names. Regan and Bodice (pronounced Bod-iss) are strong-willed and harshly calculating in their use or abuse of others. Goneril and Fontanelle are both selfish and petulantly passionate. The sisters mistrust each other and use their husbands as dispensible accessories in the struggle against Lear. Shakespeare's Cordelia is the youngest of the princesses, dutifully loving when her sisters are treacherous, compassionate when they are cruel. Bond chooses to place his Cordelia outside the royal family; she rises to prominence as a revolutionary leader. Lear is *expected* to die before the final curtain, along with Regan/ Bodice, Goneril/Fontanelle and Cordelia. Bond's Cordelia survives, although forces are gathering against her. Regan's and Goneril's husbands, the Dukes of Cornwall and Albany, are matched by Cornwall and North in Bond's play. Shakespeare allows his mad old king three companions in his desolation: The Fool, the bluntly honest nobleman, Kent, and Gloucester's too-trusting and virtuous son, Edgar. Edgar is left to pick up the reins of government. In Bond's play the Gravedigger's Boy fulfils in part the roles of Fool and Edgar, but he does not survive; it it no one individual who shoulders the burden of responsible government reassuringly just before the final curtain — Bond leaves Cordelia desperately trying to impose her idea of law and order on a battle-scarred nation while the future, in the shape of young people like Thomas and Susan, gains strength and political awareness. Bond's objective is to 'provide a meaning to the story' which will make the old tale seem relevant and truthful to a modern audience. In much the same way, Shakespeare filtered the chronicles of the Middle Ages through an essentially Tudor sensibility.

Part of the appeal of the Shakespearean epic as a model for Bond may have been the freedom it offered from the restrictions of nineteenth and twentieth century naturalism — freedom from elegant reflections of High Society, from middle-class suburban dramas, or, more recently, domestic upheavals over the kitchen sink. Many of the new plays seen on the professional stage in England from the middle of the nineteenth century up to the 1960's seem to have shared one feature: they have each moved within a very narrow social band, whether fashionably elitist, or bourgeois, or working class — consider, for example, the plays of Robertson, Pinero, Wilde, Chekhov, Galsworthy, D.H. Lawrence, Coward, Rattigan, Osborne, Pinter and Wesker. On the other hand, Shakespeare brought princes and peasants, merchants and mechanicals together in conflict or confederacy, both comic and tragic. It was possible to juxtapose the ambitions and actions of the powerful or the privileged with the effects of those actions on the common man.

Such juxtapositions could hardly escape seeming political. Henry V's stature as king — and, implicitly, the institution of kingship — is measured most effectively as he moves among his troops on the eve of battle. It is shown dramatically to be A Good Thing. In *King Lear* the oppressive cruelty of Cornwall is highlighted by the sudden gesture of protest from his servant at the blinding of Gloucester. Bond dismissed this servant's violent protest as part of 'a feudal myth', evidence of Shakespeare's political naivety and romanticism. In Bond's view it was Shakespeare's hopeful assertion that the excesses of authoritarian rule would always be tempered and checked by the stalwart decency of the common people, or rather, not by 'the common people' since the idea of massed proletarian revolt was out of tune with the Tudor respect for order and degree. Tyranny would be thwarted by an expendable individual who would then pay a heavy price for his initiative so as to discourage others from taking the law into their own hands. The system of authoritarian rule, its face once more acceptable, could then continue, confident in the divinely ordained rightness of its supremacy.

> He wants very much to believe that sort of thing, and it's not true. If a man's paid to stand by, he will stand by — there's nothing else he can do. And that is the logic of the soldier's situation, that's the sort of life that Shakespeare's life has made the soldiers live. (*Edward Bond, A Companion to the Plays*, p. 60)

Bond presents what he considers a more truthful and realistic interaction between the governors and the governed in *Lear*, Act I, scene iv, when a soldier (who is, significantly, not individualised by name but labelled with a letter) is ordered by Lear's daughters to mutilate the captured Warrington. The soldier does as he is trained and paid to do, without showing either the hysterical zest or the spitefully calculating cruelty of Fontanelle and Bodice. He shrugs off moral responsibility for his part in the atrocity: 'Don't blame me, I've got a job to do. If we were fightin' again t'morra I could end up envyin' you anytime' (p. 16). When asked what his attitude was towards this soldier — sympathy? censure? disgust? — Bond replied:

> The old religious categories of guilt and conscience seem to me to have become redundant. In a sense all acts of cruelty are signs of madness and so presumably their perpetrators shouldn't be punished for them. I'm afraid that if morality isn't a religious matter concerning god, it must be a political matter. And so justice also becomes a political matter — there is no abstract justice, no gauze over the nose to prevent buddhists destroying germs by breathing over them. There are occasions when people have to be held responsible for their individual actions because certain things have to be socially demonstrated. But really the concept of guilt is primitive and has never helped the victim. The real problem is the emancipation of society. (Letter, 4 March 1982)

This emancipation of society requires the growth to political and social maturity of these previously kept ill-informed and inarticulate within their class-confines. The theatre is to participate in the process by dramatising the problems to be confronted and by demonstrating rational solutions. In *Lear* Bond contrasts the mindless brutality of the sisters' soldiers (only possible because of the abdication of individual political responsibility involved in that authoritarian regime) with the politically conscious choice made by Ben, one-time orderly in the sisters' prisons, who has grown to maturity as a result of his own experience and Lear's teaching. Ben willingly returns to the punishment camp so that he can educate and organise others to work for the emancipation of their society. Like Lear, he may be shot down before long, but he will have, in Lear's words, 'made his mark'.

It is arguable that in *King Lear* more than in the other Shakespearean tragedies it is the story, the pattern of events, that gives the logic to characters involved; that is, the characters are propelled like chessmen from one square to another through a

complicated sequence of advances or retreats, some pieces being
quickly dismissed by the fast-moving princesses, the king finally
caught in check. The rules have to be taken as 'given': that it is,
for example, the nature of the king to begin by surrendering his
position of power; that bastard sons advance briskly by displacing
the legitimate heir and then leap forwards and sideways in
association with the attacking princesses. Goneril and Regan *are*
calculating and cruel, are never shown to have been anything else;
Edmund *is* ambitious and treacherous; Edgar *is* honest and
politically naive. These characters are revealed less through
'truthful' soliloquy than through the relationship between their
actions and the account of themselves they give to others.

There is a fairy-tale quality about Shakespeare's story of the
three daughters of an old man with an inheritance to share out, the
youngest at first discriminated against but finally shown to be the
most honourable and honoured. Perhaps it was this element which
attracted and challenged Bond, as well as the political aspect. He
adapts Shakespeare's story to suit his own needs. Bond's Cordelia
is not the youngest and loveliest of three princesses, driven into
exile by a petulant father for whom she then suffers defeat and
death. Bond emphasises and, significantly, explains the difference
between her and the other two by placing her within a different
social, economic and political context. She lives as a rural peasant,
not at court, better educated than her husband but still tied to the
land by the routines of subsistence farming. The soldiers' violation
of her home and of herself forces her to act politically; it is not
enough simply to endure. On the other hand, Shakespeare requires
the audience to take his Cordelia's motivation on trust — it is to be
accepted that, unlike her sisters, she is loyal, uncompromising and
compassionate.

Bond wants his story to seem more *rational*. In each case the
Cordelia's decision to take up arms against the two corrupt sisters
results in her own downfall: Shakespeare's heroine is defeated and
hanged in her cell; Bond's revolutionary leader becomes hardened
and harsh through the exercise of power, driving others into
political action against her. In each case Cordelia's fate may seem
unacceptably cruel, undeserved given the character's enduring
desire to do good, to do what seemed right, to battle against
tyranny.

> CORDELIA. You were here when they killed my husband. I
>   watched them kill him. I covered my face with my hands,
>   but my fingers opened so I watched. I watched them rape

me, and John kill them, and my child miscarry. I didn't
miss anything. I watched and I said we won't be at the mercy
of brutes anymore, we'll live a new life and help one another.
The government's creating that new life — you must stop
speaking against us. (*Lear*, p. 83)

> CORDELIA. . . . I yet beseech your Majesty,
> (If for I want that glib and oily art
> To speak and purpose not, since what I well intend,
> I'll do't before I speak), that you make known
> It is no vicious blot, murther or foulness,
> No unchaste action, or dishonour's step,
> That hath depriv'd me of your grace and favour,
> But even for want of that for which I am richer,
> A still-soliciting eye, and such a tongue
> That I am glad I have not, though not to have it
> Hath lost me in your liking. (*King Lear*, I i, 222-232)

In Bond's play it is less important to feel sympathy for Cordelia's
situation as oppressor-to-be-toppled than to recognise why she has
become so: Lear, with his hard-won wisdom, is able to explain so
that the lesson is not lost even if the character called Cordelia
cannot see the truth.

> LEAR. Listen, Cordelia. You have two enemies, lies *and* the
> truth. You sacrifice truth to destroy lies, and you sacrifice
> life to destroy death. It isn't sane. [. . .] But I've learned this,
> and you must learn it or you'll die. Listen, Cordelia. If a God
> had made the world, might would always be right, that
> would be so wise, we'd be spared so much suffering. But we
> made the world — out of our smallness and weakness. Our
> lives are awkward and fragile and we have only one thing
> to keep us sane: pity, and the man without pity is mad.
> [. . .] Your Law always does more harm than crime, and
> your morality is a form of violence. (*Lear*, pp. 84-85)

Shakespeare, on the other hand, stresses the helplessness of his
Cordelia in the face of a grim reality:

> CORDELIA. . . . We are not the first
> Who with best meaning, have incurr'd the worst.
> For thee, oppressed King, I am cast down;
> Myself could else out-frown false Fortune's frown. (*King
> Lear*, V iii, 3-6)

Lear

During the months of preparation for *Lear* (1969-70) Bond worked towards his final form through a series of essays and poems on related issues. He started not from a response to Shakespeare's *King Lear* but to Chekhov's *Three Sisters*, which he translated for the Royal Court in 1967, and from a determination to find some way to dramatise the conflict and contrast he saw between the demands of justice and of law and order. In his diaries in December of 1969 he wrote:

> Why *Lear* and *Three Sisters*? *Three Sisters* partly because they've stayed in my mind since I translated them. Why *Lear*? Partly because of the moral imbalance . . . if you look at these three girls, you'll find they all suffer as much and die like Lear, and are no more guilty than him — that in fact, they are like the three sisters. (Hay and Roberts, *Bond*, p. 107)

He was, however, concerned that his play should not be seen merely as an updating of Shakespeare and Chekhov, that it should have 'a structure rooted in itself'. His notes reveal the stages through which his structure evolved, defining the crucial areas of difference between *his* intentions and the message he saw in *King Lear*. Instead of abdication at the start, in his play there is revolution. Successive conflicts bring different leaders into power, but that power crushes their humanity and compassion — it threatens freedom in the name of law and order — so that for the mass of the people nothing really changes. The first part of Shakespeare's play dramatises moments of choice or deliberate reaction in Lear: he chooses to abdicate; he chooses to reject Cordelia in favour of Regan and Goneril; he dictates the terms of his retirement; he chooses to leave Goneril's house rather than compromise; he chooses to leave Gloucester's castle and seek the storm. As Cornwall remarks: ' 'Tis best to give him way; he leads himself' (II iv). His madness leaves him weak; he no longer tries to dictate the pattern of events and thus the movement of the scenes alters. When he wakes from his long sleep to find Cordelia beside him, he is engulfed by self-pity and doubt:

> I am mightily abus'd. I should e'en die with pity
> To see another thus. I know not what to say. (*King Lear*, IV
> vii, 53-54)

He has no interest in resisting his capture by Edmund since he is wholly absorbed in his relationship with Cordelia. He plays no part in his release and is unable to prevent Cordelia's death. Finally, his own death has no significance for him beyond the ending of his life — he does not actively seek it nor show any understanding of its political importance.

Bond's play reverses this processs. His Lear does not choose to surrender power and status; they are wrested from him. His apparent madness and retreat into a nightmare world of tortured images is a phase through which he reaches a more rational understanding of his situation and can *act* morally — that is, in Bond's terms, in a politically responsible way. He then chooses to defy Cordelia; he chooses to leave his sanctuary with Thomas and Susan, and to accept the obligations and opportunities incumbent upon him uniquely because of what he has been, a king, and because of what he has involuntarily become — high priest, prophet and scourge of Cordelia's administration. As Bond says:

> Lear discovers something in himself, out of this comes his ability to act. He 'understands' at last and has the 'arrogance of truth and simplicity'. (*Theatre Quarterly*, Vol. II, No. 5, 1972, p. 27)

It is not important that Lear's action cannot instantly effect change and restore humanity and compassion to the processes of government; he is no Shakespearean Prince Hal translated into Henry V in time to guarantee a Golden Age, nor, like Richmond at the end of *Richard III*, the founder of a new dynasty victorious on Bosworth Field. Not even an Edgar, sadder and wiser than before, but still young enough to pick up the tools of government and start rebuilding a nation. Bond's Lear makes a solitary assault on the Wall (which has become a symbol for the kind of implacable paternalism practised by him at first and Cordelia later), and this action is important because it demonstrates a way out of the present predicament, what Bond referred to in the play's Preface as 'a *method* of change' rather than a 'plan of the future'. In some of the *Theatre Poems and Songs*, written partly as steps on the way to the completion of *Lear* and partly as a commentary, Bond has underlined the phases and key images which give shape to the play:

> Lear was born in ancient shadow
> When men stumbled in darkness
> And bound their wounds with myths

In scene one Lear suffers the Great Vice
Fear
And so commits the Three Great Grimes
Cruelty arrogance and rhetoric

He's shot on the wall
At death he began to make a new life
Others still live the old life

[. . .] Our world is not absurd — our society is
Art is rational and subverts the past
When the weak choose to fight they are already strong
A man's pessimism is measured by what he will lose
His hope by what he will gain
When the world is changed

This play is guerilla in the theatre. [. . .] (pp. 3-4)

The two sisters

Despite Bond's criticism of what he judged to be an evasion of
political issues in *King Lear*, he was evidently interested by the
self-destruction of the family which was bound up with the
violation of the nation. His wish to examine 'the *causes* of human
misery and the *sources* of human strength' rather than to accept
misery and power as given factors in men's lives is expressed in his
relatively sympathetic verdict on Goneril and Regan. He cannot
view them as motivelessly malignant, the two ugly sisters in a fairy
tale. In his interpretation of the story Bond tries to dramatise the
reasons behind the conflict within the family. Shakespeare shows
Regan and Goneril shifting from a public profession of loving
respect for their father to actions of personal rejection and finally
to the military and political opposition which destroys them all.
Through Kent, Cordelia and the Fool, Shakespeare indicates from
the outset that Goneril's and Regan's declarations of filial love and
duty are spurious, so that their quick impatience with Lear's
demands for continuing deference and indulgence for himself and
his retinue is expected and consistent:

GONERIL. Sir, I love you more than word can wield the
matter; Dearer than eye-sight, space and liberty. (*King Lear*,
I i, 54-55)

(The reference to eye-sight becomes grimly resonant in this play
and in Bond's.)

REGAN. I am made of that self metal as my sister,
    And prize me at her worth. In my true heart
    I find she names my very deed of love;
    Only she comes too short . . . (*King Lear*, I i, 68-71)

The imagery describes the quality of their existence — they are already cast in their mould, both of one metal and determined by its qualities. No explanations: they *are* what they are, 'glib and oily', full of 'plighted cunning'. Only for Cordelia is it suggested that she is the product of her up-bringing, her environment and education:

    'You have begot me, bred me, lov'd me . . .' (*King Lear*, I i, 97)

Nonetheless, it is not explained *why* she should have been cast in purer and softer metal than her sisters. Certainly Lear's autocratic behaviour, his wish to wrench the world to fit his whims, his unreasonable demands for the pomp and privilege of power without the associated responsibilities, and his insensitivity to the needs of the people around him all provide a context for his elder daughters' wilfulness, selfishness and lack of humanity. He, however, cannot recognise his contribution to his daughters' characters. 'Are you our daughter?' he asks Goneril when she first complains about the behaviour of his attendants (I iv). He threatens her with barrenness. Beyond Cordelia's reference to her own growing-up, there is little dramatic life given to the idea of Lear as a father to very young daughters. The emphasis in *King Lear* is, rather, on what divides them; as the Fool remarks: 'I marvel what kin thou and thy daughters are' (I iv, 178). Of course, a past is *implied* that might explain the miseries and the conflicts of the play's present, but the movement and the manner of the action and the language impel the audience's attention forwards towards the final catastrophe.

    Bond shows Bodice and Fontanelle similarly moving from decorous involvement in the performance of public duties to the explicit opposition to Lear which leads to their own ruin. He shows their revolt as a consequence of their up-bringing — they have grown to fear not to love their overbearing father, and they have been brought up in a system of privilege and an atmosphere of violence which have taught them to act with brutal selfishness. Fontanelle greets the moment of open conflict with relief: 'Happiness at last! I was always terrified of him!' (p. 8). Bond's Lear, like Shakespeare's, tries to dissociate himself from his daughters: 'I have no daughters' (p. 6). He speaks of their sexuality with disgust and predicts that their selfishness will make them barren.

> I knew it would come to this! I knew you were malicious!
> I built my wall against you as well as my other enemies! You
> talk of marriage? You have murdered your family. There will
> be no more children. Your husbands are impotent . . . I've
> watched you scheme and plan — they'll lie by you when you
> dream! (p. 6)

Nonetheless, he harks back with nostalgia to their childhood, to an image of them as vulnerable and affectionate, needing his care and protection. In prison after his capture by their troops, he summons up the ghosts of Bodice and Fontanelle as young girls, fondles them and tries to reassure them (II ii). Bodice and Fontanelle are seen as anxious to please their father who is a remote firure, often away from his family in the pursuit of power and political security, and whose appearances are special occasions:

> FONTANELLE. Do my hair . . . Father comes home today.
>   (p. 38)

Bodice, even as a child, is preoccupied by images of power, the power-politics that bring death home with Lear: 'Father's brought the coffins on carts' (p. 38). Fontanelle's and Lear's chance of tenderness is wrecked by Fontanelle's preoccupation with her appearance as she struggles into her dress. Then Bodice appals Lear by putting on her dead mother's dress: 'My poor child, you might as well have worn her shroud' (p. 39). An absent father, a dead mother — the young girls have had no-one to teach them that life has more to it than rivalry for power and legalised violence. When the real world breaks into Lear's image of the past with the entry of soldiers to search his cell, Lear cannot hold on to the vision despite his cry: 'We can stay here together' (p. 41). This image of the children and their father in Lear's cell dramatically relates the past to the play's present. The family has always been walled in by the realities of politics. They have had only an illusion of freedom. These tyrannies of power link Bodice and Cordelia. Bodice was born to 'greatness'; Cordelia has it thrust violently upon her — but the result is much the same.

> BODICE. My decisions are forced on me. I change people's lives
>   and things get done — it's like a mountain moving forward,
>   but not because I tell it to. [. . .] I hated being a girl, but at
>   least I was happy sometimes. And it was better when I grew

up, I could be by myself — they didn't humiliate me then. I
was almost free! I made so many plans, one day I'd be my
own master! Now I have all the power . . . and I'm a slave.
(pp. 48-9)

For Cordelia, too, the need to *govern* becomes an inescapable
imperative:

CORDELIA. Yes, you sound like the voice of my conscience.
But if you listened to everything your conscience told you,
you'd go mad. You'd never get anything done — and there's a
lot to do, some of it very hard.
LEAR. Don't build the wall.
CORDELIA. We must. [. . .]
LEAR. The wall will destroy you. It's already doing it. How can
I make you see? [. . .]
CORDELIA. In this situation a good government acts strongly.
(pp. 84-5)

Bodice's ability to see what power is doing to her perhaps makes
her a more sympathetic figure despite the atrocities she has been
responsible for. She has had moments of happiness; she *feels* the
lost opportunities, has glimpsed a kind of freedom only to lose it.
That sense of waste and loss is also conveyed in Act II, scene vi,
when Fontanelle is captured and shot. Her terror flings her back
into childlike responses: 'Help me, father . . . What will you say to
them?' (p.57). Bond dramatises what Shakespeare keeps as an idea.
Shakespeare's Lear in his madness cries out: 'Then let them
anatomize Regan, see what breeds about her heart.' (III vi, 74). In
Bond's *Lear* Fontanelle is actually cut open, and as Lear looks at
her body he sees her with a new tenderness; he recognises what she
might have been and so feels truly bereaved:

If I had known she was so beautiful . . . Her body was made by
the hand of a child, so sure and nothing unclean . . . If I had
known this beauty and patience and care, how I would have
loved her. Did I make this — and destroy it? (p. 59)

Regan and Goneril are allowed no such final softness.

ALBANY. Produce the bodies, be they alive or dead;
This judgement of the heavens, that makes us tremble,
Touches us not with pity. (*King Lear*, V iii, 229-231)

The Gravedigger's Boy

In Shakespeare's play, the treacherous rhetoric of Regan and
Goneril and the self-delusions of Lear are put into perspective not
only by Cordelia's and Kent's ungarnished honesty but also by the
mordant wit of the Fool. The character of the witty Fool is present
in many of Shakespeare's plays — Touchstone in *As You Like It*,
for example, and Feste in *Twelfth Night*. He exists on the fringes
of life at court, licensed by his jester's livery to mock the
affectations and vices of his masters through songs, puns, riddles
and mimicry. King Lear's Fool is first referred to in Act 1, scene iii,
when Goneril seizes upon an incident involving him and the king as
the final straw breaking the back of her grudging endurance of her
father and his retinue. That is, the Fool and Lear are in alliance
against what the audience already knows to be despicable. When
Lear feels rebuffed by Goneril it is the Fool he calls for, yet in
their first presented encounter the Fool tries to make Lear
recognise the nature and extent of his folly, not maliciously but
because he cares for the old man. Lear, however, cannot see the
relevance of the Fool's comments to his own situation.

> LEAR. Dost thou call me fool, boy?
> FOOL. All thy other titles thou hast given away; that thou wast
> born with. (*King Lear*, I iv, 145-47)

In Bond's play the Gravedigger's Boy at first performs a similar
function: that is, he appears when Lear is displaced and threatened
and he shows pity to the old man, seeming to provide an alternative
to the father-child bond which has proved so damaging both to
Lear and to his daughters:

> BOY. He can't look after himself. He's a poor old man — how
> can I throw him out? Who'd look after him then? I won't
> do it. (p. 21)

At this point he sees Lear simply as an old man in need of help, not
as a king who represents an unworkable political system and wields
power irresponsibly. Like Shakespeare's Fool, however, the Boy
offers a critical picture of Lear's arrogance, blindness and folly as
king, using a succession of vivid images:

> BOY. The king was mad. He took all the men from this village.
> But I hid. They'd worked with their hands all their lives but
> when they started on the wall their hands bled for a week.
> LEAR. No.

BOY. You died of work or they shot you for not working.
    There was a disease —
LEAR. They tried to stop that.
BOY. — 'Wall death'. Their feet used to swell with the mud. The
    stink of it even when you were asleep! Living in a grave! He
    should come here — I'd go back to my old job and dig a
    grave for him! (p. 25)

There is a double irony here. The Boy cannot recognise the mad
king in the old man before him, so Lear and his political identity
are disengaged briefly and placed side by side for comparison. Then
there is the irony of the Boy's situation: he successfully hid from
Lear's soldiers when men from his village were being taken to work
and to die on the Wall, yet at that moment he invites into his
refuge the same mad king whose presence will lead to his own
violent death and the rape of his wife. Bond's Lear, like
Shakespeare's, resists the truth being presented to him, but he is
pushed towards a realisation of his real plight, expressed at first as
dreams or in fantastic images:

LEAR. There was a king and he had a fountain in his garden. It
    was as big as the sea. One night the fountain howled and in
    the morning the king went to look at it. It was red. The
    servants emptied it and under the sea they found a desert.
    The king looked in the sand and there was a helmet and
    sword. (p. 26)

Not only does the Gravedigger's Boy play in part the role of Fool,
he also contains elements of Shakespeare's Edgar. When Edgar
assumes the guise of poor mad Tom, cast out from society, a
ragged thing unable to communicate effectively with any but the
mad Lear, he moves Lear to pity since his plight seems to rival
Lear's own and his helplessness to be even greater. This is one step
on Lear's journey towards some kind of rehabilitation — it starts
to break through his egotism. The Gravedigger's Boy not only
shows pity himself towards the old king, but, perhaps more
valuably, he teaches Lear to *feel* pity — not a generalised and largely
rhetorical pity for oppressed humanity en masse, but pity directed
towards specific pain, a response to another's immediate need. In
prison, the emaciated and disorientated ghost of the Boy clings to
Lear:

GHOST. I'm afraid. Let me stay with you, keep me here, please.
LEAR. Yes yes. Poor boy. Lie down by me. Here. I'll hold you.

> We'll help each other. Cry while I sleep, and I'll cry and
> watch you while you sleep. We'll take turns. The sound of
> the human voice will comfort us. (p. 42)

The Ghost makes Lear understand his personal responsibility for
the suffering of others and his need to try to make amends:

> LEAR. He was very good to me. He saved my mind when I went
>   mad. And to tell you the truth I did him a great wrong once,
>   a very great wrong. He's never blamed me. I must be kind to
>   him now. (p. 54)

The intense pathos of the relationship between Lear and the Ghost
helps to humanise Bond's political epic, to add an important
dimension to the 'meaning' that the character of Lear is to
communicate to the audience. However, the Ghost's vain effort to
hide from the political realities of the kingdom in which he lived,
and the temptation he offers to Lear to retreat from action into a
selfishly sentimental pastoral idyll represent an attitude which
Bond demonstrates is unacceptable:

> GHOST. I'd have led you about and watched you grow old,
>   your beautiful old age . . . (p. 82)

After his confrontation with Cordelia, Lear knows that the Ghost
will only sap his will and prevent him from realising his potential
for rational action:

> LEAR. You must die! I love you, I'll always remember you, but
>   I can't help you. Die, for your own sake die! (p. 86)

So, too, in *King Lear* the Fool fades from the scene once Lear has
to find his own way back from madness into the real world to meet
Cordelia properly and to suffer the political consequences of his
earlier irresponsibility — civil war and the death of those he loves.
It is not really clear whether the Fool simply gets pushed into the
background or whether he, like Cordelia, is murdered. When Lear
says (V iii, 304): 'And my poor fool is hang'd!', it could refer
either to the Fool or to Cordelia herself. It is not important to
know — more important is the recognition that there is no longer
any role for the Fool to play; he is not needed to guide his 'poor
nuncle' to reconciliation with Cordelia, any more than, in Bond's
play, the Ghost is needed at Lear's final assault on the Wall.
Nonetheless, the Boy and his Ghost are an essential part of Lear's
journey from political and moral blindness towards awareness and
action. Bond emphasised this when he was involved in the Royal

Court Theatre's production of *Lear* in 1971.

> [Lear] has to disown something of himself, this instinctive thing
> he calls the Gravedigger's Boy. That, incidentally, was the image
> from which the play grew — this image of the Gravedigger's
> Boy. In some senses he is much older than Lear, and Lear
> recognizes this — he has been in his grave, and Lear, who is a
> very old man, has still to go towards it. (*Theatre Quarterly*,
> Vol. 11, No. 5, Jan-March 1972, p. 8)

Rhetoric: the language of Lear

Rhetoric is one of Lear's Three Great Crimes, according to Bond.
In the early scenes of Bond's play the rhetoric is used to defend
what Bond describes as a myth, which asserts that Might is Right
and that Law and Order are legitimately weapons in the hands of
strong government. In his essay, 'Politics and the English Language',
Orwell linked abuse of language with abuse of power:

> In our time, political speech and writing are largely the defence
> of the indefensible [. . .] Thus political language has to consist
> largely of euphemism, question-begging and sheer cloudy
> vagueness. [. . .] The great enemy of clear language is insincerity.
> (*Shooting an Elephant and Other Essays*, pp. 96-7)

Lear, Bodice and Cordelia, the Old Councillor and Warrington are
all required to defend the indefensible:

> LEAR. My wall will make you free. . . . (p. 3)

> WARRINGTON. Nothing's gained by being firm in little matters
> . . . (p. 6)

> BODICE. This is a political trial: politics is the higher form of
> justice . . . (p. 32)

> 4th PRISONER. Then he could be made politically ineffective
> . . . (p. 62)

> COUNCILLOR. Like many of my colleagues I gave the new
> undertaking of loyalty. I've always tried to serve people. I
> see that as my chief duty. If we abandon the administration
> there'd be chaos. (p. 78)

The newly wise Lear's comment on this is unambivalent: 'You
comit crimes and call them law! . . . Power has spoken' (p. 78).

Shakespeare's Lear also begins with a rhetorical defence of an
action that events prove to have been indefensible. Regan and

Goneril use rhetoric to gain power, while Cordelia's failure of
rhetoric is cruelly punished: 'Nothing will come of nothing: speak
again'. The 'oily glibness' of the elder daughters' speeches signals
the travesty of justice that is being perpetrated in the name of
Lear's 'darker purpose' and 'largest bounty'. The extravagantly
sentimental or pretentious imagery echoes ominously, since
evidently it cannot be an accurate or sincere expression of the
characters' feelings. Cordelia's directness sets the standard of true
utterance by which the integrity of the others can be judged. Their
language is heightened and formal. Bond has not only adapted the
epic structure and scope of Shakespeare's theatre for his own
purposes; he has also exploited the possibilities inherent in the
epic style — freedom from naturalism making way for vivid
imagery, oratory, parables and overtly theatrical statements and
gestures. His Lear, for example, uses the emotive imagery of the
New Testament to trick out his self-justification:

> When I'm dead my people will live in freedom and peace and
> remember my name, no — venerate it! . . . They are my sheep
> and if one of them is lost I'd take fire to hell to bring him out.
> I loved and cared for my children, and now you've sold them to
> my enemies! (p. 7)

This rhetoric of love and Christ-like paternalism is immediately
exploded by a gunshot as Lear summarily executes one of his
'sheep', a worker from the Wall.

The political rhetoric of these characters is recognisable and
placeable, but it is in its turn only one element of the rhetoric of
the play as a whole. 'A propaganda play must be able to tell its
message to an uninformed or resisting audience.' (*The Worlds*,
p. 128) The 'telling' involves such instruments of persuasion as
emotive imagery, ironic juxtapositions, startling gestures, violent
action and poignant sentimentality, and the borrowed authority of
time-honoured myths and legends and creeds. The message of *Lear*
is unambiguously stated in some of the related poems. For example:

> *To the Audience*
> You sit and watch the stage
> Your back is turned —
> To what?
>
> The firing squad
> Shoots in the back of the neck
> Whole nations have been caught
> Looking the wrong way

I want to remind you
Of what you forgot to see
On the way here
To listen to what
You were too busy to hear
To ask you to believe
What you were too ashamed to admit

If what you see on the stage displeases
You run away
Lucky audience!
Is there no innocence in chains
In the world you run to?
No child starving
Because your world's too weak
And all the rich too poor
To feed it?

On the stage actors talk of life and imitate death
You must solve their problems in your life
I remind you
They show future deaths (*Theatre Poems and Songs,* p. 4)

In the play itself Bond employs a recognisably Elizabethan and Jacobean range of dramatic rhetoric. 'Rhetoric' describes language or gesture which is designed to have a specific effect on the hearer or spectator. There is the rhetoric of stage violence — the blinding of Gloucester in Shakespeare's *King Lear* is matched by the removal of Lear's eyes in Bond's play. There is the rhetoric of pathos — Shakespeare's Cordelia borne in by the heart-broken old king finds an echo in the ghost of the Boy dying for a second time in the arms of Bond's Lear. Bond also uses ghosts and visions to dramatise and heighten his characters' inner turmoil in a manner reminiscent of Shakespeare and of Shakespeare's contemporary, John Webster (c. 1580-c. 1625). He has, like the Elizabethan playwright Christopher Marlowe (1564-93), a flair for powerful stage metaphor or image-making: the machinery of Lear's blinding presented with the 4th Prisoner's tone of professional benevolence recalls the assassin Lightborn's relish in the mysteries of his art at the murder of the imprisoned king in Marlowe's *Edward II* (1591).

Bond's range of language in *Lear* can emulate the Jacobeans' combination of the poetic and the prosaic as a vehicle for the play's message. They share a vividness of imagery. Shakespeare, for example, gives expression to the unnatural cruelty of Regan and

Goneril, on the one hand, and to the natural, fragile innocence of
Cordelia, on the other, through images drawn from nature. The
sisters' ingratitude is 'sharper than the serpent's tooth'; they are
'pelican daughters'. Lear and Cordelia in captivity will 'sing like
birds i' th' cage'. That image of a caged creature is also eloquently
used by Bond to heighten the pathos of his Lear's passionate
frenzy in Act Two:

> No, that's not the king . . . This is a little cage of bars with an
> animal in it. No, no, that's not the King! Who shut that animal
> in that cage. Let it out. Have you seen its face behind the bars?
> There's a poor animal with blood on its head and tears running
> down its face. (p. 35)

The highly charged nature of the image makes Bodice's response
extraordinarily shocking: 'Yes! I've locked this animal in its cage
and I will not let it out!' (p. 35)

Bond's use of language is both dramatic and poetic, in a line of
descent from Shakespeare through the poet and visionary, William
Blake (1757-1827). There will be little doubt that Bodice has put
all Heaven in a Rage if one remembers Blake's 'Auguries of
Innocence':

> A Robin Red breast in a Cage
> Puts all Heaven in a Rage [. . .]
> A dog starved at his Master's Gate
> Predicts the ruin of the State.

Bond not only echoes Blake's imagery but also the deceptively
simple moral creed voiced in the 'Auguries of Innocence':

> A truth that's told with bad intent
> Beats all the Lies you can invent [. . .]
> The Beggar's Rags fluttering in Air
> Does to Rags the Heavens tear.

This strong connection with the religious poetry of Blake indicates
one reason for Bond's use of stories and images from the Bible —
the Bible is a powerful element in many people's inherited culture,
using images taken from common experience (family life, eating
and drinking, building, farming) to communicate a Rule of Life or
moral code. Its authority is bolstered by the faith of generations.
In Bond's play, Lear welcomes confidence tricksters and deserters,
sinners in need of salvation, during the period when he is playing
the role of sage and saviour of a sickly flock. He says to Thomas

and Susan: 'I came here when I was cold and hungry and afraid. I wasn't turned away, and I won't turn anyone away' (p. 74). This echoes Christ's words — 'I was hungry and you fed me, naked and you clothed me . . .'. Lear also uses parables to teach the crowds who come to hear him (pp. 74-75), and is both presented to and protected from these people by his closest disciples, much as Jesus is said to have been. The Biblical idiom may challenge an audience's assumptions about Lear's status, or waken deep-seated responses.

In contrast to the poetic and Biblical elements, Bond's style can be earthy and prosaic: 'Oe else yer got knockin' around?' (p. 42). It can also be crisply witty; some of its humorously balanced statements hark back to the epigrams of the poet and playwright Oscar Wilde (1854-1900) as well as forward to Bond's later play, *Restoration* (1981).

> BODICE. Men are always obstinate, it's their form of maturity.
> (p. 36)

> BODICE. Victory is bad for soldiers, it lowers their morale.
> (p. 37)

Significantly Bond gives such neatly turned phrases to characters whose hypocrisy and abuse of authority he intends to expose and condemn. They are implicated in what Bond sees as the false culture of the entrenched Establishment.

It is thus mistaken to think of Bond as naive stylistically, his work 'unshaped by the hand of art' as J.W. Lambert put it in his review of *Saved*. He may have left school with relief as soon as possible, but the width and intensity of his reading is well reflected in the range and sophistication of the language of *Lear*.

Ideas to be enacted

> In a play ideas must be enacted and not simply spoken. [. . .]
> In a play the value of an idea isn't in its literal sense but in the relation a character has to his idea, and the play must show the character bearing the responsibility of having such an idea or such a belief. The play makes a judgement, and the ability to make and understand such judgements is the centre of all education. (From a note issued with the programme of the Royal Court *Lear*.)

Woven into the dominant political argument of *Lear* are a number of distinct strands, ideas which are defined and developed through their relation to various characters. Often these ideas are seen in opposing or in complementary pairs: Seeing-Blindness, Freedom-Imprisonment, Loyalty-Betrayal, Justice-Law and Order, Madness-Sanity, Power-Subjugation, Innocence-Responsibility (sometimes, more explicitly, Guilt). Some words, or ideas, recur frequently, given changing shades of irony through their relation to the speaker on the one hand, and to the situation on the other. Consider, for example, 'conscience'. Fontanelle asserts: 'I'll only sign what doesn't conflict with my conscience' (p. 47) — then signs her father's death warrant, apparently oblivious of the implied comment on her personal morality. Cordelia bitterly remarks that Lear sounds like the voice of her conscience, condemning her efforts to govern the country strongly: 'But if you listened to everything your conscience told you you'd go mad' (p. 83). Yet she thinks of herself as representing the forces of right working to fulfil her hope that 'we'll live a new life and help one another'. The Old Councillor, testifying against the king to whom he had once sworn loyalty but whom he had opportunistically deserted in defeat, claims: 'I did my duty as a man of conscience' (p. 34).

'Duty', 'conscience' — Bond demonstrates the dangerous plausibility yet instability of such concepts through these different relationships of word to character and action. 'Justice', too, is a recurring theme, the word being used to clothe with respectability the perversion of law or to lend authority to a bid for survival. At the start of the play Bodice protests at the summary execution of a worker from the Wall: 'Father, if you kill this man it will be an injustice' (p. 4). There is an irony, therefore, when at the beginning of Act Two she declares 'politics is the higher form of justice' (p. 32) as she suborns the judge who is to pass sentence on Lear. A further irony is added when Bodice tries to escape the death ordered for her by Cordelia and the carpenter: 'I have a right to justice in court!' (p. 61). The irony lies in the word's reverberations of which the speaker appears unaware, yet the audience should become increasingly alert to such echoes and implications. It is through stimulating this kind of growing awareness that Bond intends to educate his audiences, first to make them aware and then to make them politically active.

The enactment of an idea in the theatre can have a physical immediacy which the words alone do not possess. The idea of 'Seeing and Blindness' is insistent in *Lear*, as in *King Lear*. Bodice's first speech is appropriate to the occasion — a tour of inspection round the Wall — but her words raise a thematic question which recurs often: 'We needn't go on. We can see the end' (p. 2). If she

and Fontanelle really could 'see the end', any further action on
their part might well seem pointless – why travel further towards
catastrophe? In fact, her inability to see is conveyed by her
confidence that she knows how things are and where they are
leading. In the same scene, Lear tries to explain away his daughters'
challenge to his authority in terms of blindness:

> You're like blind children. Can't you see they only want to get
> over the Wall? (p. 6)

In making a connection between blindness to political realities and
a physical blindness, Bond has followed a pattern set from the
beginning of *King Lear*:

> LEAR. Out of my sight!
> KENT. See better, Lear; and let me still remain
>   The true blank of thine eye. (I i, 156-158)

When Lear is forced to recognise Goneril's hostile rejection of him,
he says:

> LEAR. Old fond eyes,
>   Beweep this cause again, I'll pluck ye out,
>   And cast you, with the waters that you loose,
>   To temper clay. (I iv, 299-301)

Gloucester justifies helping Lear to escape from Regan and Goneril:

> GLOUCESTER. Because I would not see
>   Thy cruel nails pluck out his poor old eyes.
>   [. . .] but I shall see
>   The winged vengeance overtake such children.
> CORNWALL. See't shalt thou never. Fellows, hold the chair.
>   Upon these eyes of thine I'll set my foot. (III vii, 54-55,
>   63-66)

Suddenly the metaphor becomes action as Cornwall gouges out
Gloucester's eyes, an idea violently enacted and shocking on a level
beyond the intellectual or the literary. The audience become
witnesses to the event - either moved to protest, or silently passive
as accomplices in Cornwall's inhumanity. But Gloucester's physical
blindness forces him to reflect more clearly upon his experiences
and to recognise truths he had overlooked before.

> OLD MAN. You cannot see your way.
> GLOUCESTER. I have no way, and therefore want no eyes;
>   I stumbled when I saw. (IV i, 17-19)

And even Lear, in his distraction, understands that 'A man may see how the world goes with no eyes' (IV vi, 148).

Bond explores the possibilities of blindness as a metaphor and represents the idea theatrically, as, for example, through the blind old sailor led in to give evidence at Lear's trial:

> OLD SAILOR. I will tell the truth. I can't see. I was a sailor and the sea blinded me. [. . .] I've been blind seven years, sir. They say I have clear eyes, but they don't see for me.
> (pp. 33-34)

It is gently done here, a satisfyingly neat way of raising doubts about the conventional methods of establishing proofs in law — a blind man is to identify the king. As the play progresses, however, the metaphor of blindness becomes more harshly realised, its political importance underlined in terms of Lear's autocratic rule:

> LEAR. I shouldn't have looked. I killed so many people and never looked at one of their faces. (p. 42)

Then Bond translates the idea into violent action, as Shakespeare did with the blinding of Gloucester — Lear's eyes are removed by another political prisoner, with a device 'perfected on dogs for removing human eyes' (p. 63). The event is calculatedly shocking: first Lear is coaxed into a straitjacket — an idea earlier proved potent in Strindberg's play, *The Father* (1887) — and a contraption is lowered over his head. The formality and the deliberation of the actions heighten the horror since the audience have time to understand the reality behind the 4th Prisoner's comment to the carpenter: 'Then he could be made politically ineffective' (p. 62). There is time, also, to anticipate and imagine the refinements of pain to be inflicted on Lear, and to cringe at Lear's terror:

> No, no. You mustn't touch my eyes. I must have my eyes.
> (p. 63)

Bond allows no softening of the event. Lear screams in agony as the 4th Prisoner proudly describes the details of the procedure. That the moment can be theatrically powerful is clear from the response of critics to each production of the play. For example, the Royal Shakespeare Company's production of *Lear* in 1982 met with critical respect for Bond's ambitious choice of subject and for the moments of lyricism in the play, but there was also a fascinated unease about the enacted violence.

Mr. Bond has made it yet more gruesome than Shakespeare by stripping the scene of passion and framing it in a cool medical context. [. . .] Lear is to be incapacitated for expediency, and the eyes are sucked out to plop with a plonk into vials of fluid. (Ned Chaillet, *The Times*, 1.7.1982)

Bond's own strong artistic and intellectual personality is everywhere apparent. His horrors are more numerous than Shakespeare's. What with rape, mutilations, shootings, ghosts and mental tortures, this might seem more like *Titis Andronicus* than *King Lear*. (Stanley Wells, *T.L.S.*, 16.7.1982)

However, if the horror were somehow diluted, rendered aesthetically decorous, the purpose or meaning of Bond's epic story would become blurred. Partly as an answer to the squeamishness of his critics, Bond wrote in the Preface to *Lear*:

I write about violence as naturally as Jane Austen wrote about manners. Violence shapes and obsesses our society, and if we do not stop being violent we have no future. People who do not want writers to write about violence want to stop them writing about our time. It would be immoral not to write about violence.

The horrific events in *Lear* are involved in Bond's thesis that men are not necessarily or innately violent, but are driven to react violently when they feel trapped within an irrational and inhumane political system or when they are too frightened to admit the possibility of change and so struggle viciously to preserve the status quo. Bond insists in his Preface that even a play such as *Lear*, which shows the darkest side of man's experience, is not full of despair:

There is no need for pessimism or resignation, and this play is certainly not either of these things. Lear is blind till they take his eyes away, and by then he has begun to see, to understand.

If the process stopped there, at Lear's recognition of his true relationship with the society he inhabits, then the play would stop short of its rational consummation — political action. Bond explained the intention of the play's final image: Lear's assault on the Wall is a positive action not a gesture of despair.

I think of Lear as being the object and the Gravedigger's Boy as being, in a way, almost, his reflection under him — as if Lear were standing in a puddle or beside a stream. So that when Lear

digs on top of the Wall he is doing the grave-digging activity in
reverse. He is, as it were, digging out (in the sense of digging
away) a grave that has been erected in the sky — that is one way
he could look at the Wall. The Gravedigger's Boy becomes a
creature of death who inhabits a grave — Lear at the end is
destroying (by a reinterpretation of life, which has to become a
ground of action for his 'party') a living grave. (Letter,
16 September 1982)

Lear at the end of the play. Royal Court, 1971.

Further reading

Bond's own work

Plays: 1 (*Saved, Early Morning, The Pope's Wedding*), 1997

Plays: 2 (*Lear, The Sea, Narrow Road to the Deep North, Black Mass, Passion*), 1978

Plays: 3 (*Bingo, The Fool, The Woman*), 1987

Plays: 4 (*The Worlds, The Activists Papers, Restoration, Summer*), 1992

Plays: 5 (*Human Cannon, The Bundle, Jackets, In the Company of Men*), 1996

Plays: 6 (*The War Plays – Red Black and Ignorant, The Tin Can People, Great Peace; Choruses from After the Assassinations*), 1998

Plays: 7 (*Olly's Prison, Coffee, The Crime of the Twenty-First Century, The Swing, Derek, Fables and Stories*), 2003

Plays: 8 (*Born, People, Chair, Existence, The Under Room*), 2006

Some of the plays are also available in individual editons, including:

A-A-America! & Stone, 1976; revised 1981

At the Inland Sea, 1997

Eleven Vests & Tuesday, 1997

The Children & Have I None, 2000

Also published:

Theatre Poems and Songs, 1978

Poems 1978–1985

Selections from the Notebooks of Edward Bond (two volumes), 2000–1

The Hidden Plot: Notes on Theatre and the State, 2000

Writing about Bond's work

T. Coult, *The Plays of Edward Bond* (Methuen, London, 1978): a good introduction to Bond's early plays, written in a direct, unacademic style with the material organised under thematic headings.

M. Hay and P. Roberts, *Edward Bond: A Companion to the Plays*

(TQ Publications, London, 1978): a very useful reference book for all Bond material up to mid-1978, providing a chronology, a comprehensive bibliography, articles and letters written by Bond about his plays, and a record of all professional productions of the plays in Britain and abroad up to 1978.

M. Hay and P. Roberts, *Bond: a Study of his Plays* (Methuen, London, 1980): a detailed discussion of the origins, development, concerns and style of Bond's plays up to and including *The Bundle* and *The Woman*. It also contains a full bibliography for those with a specialist interest.

David L. Hirst, *Edward Bond* (Macmillan, Basingstoke, 1985)

C. Marowitz, *Confessions of a Counterfeit Critic* (Methuen, London, 1973): reprints his review of *Early Morning* and *Lear*.

Jenny S. Spencer, *Dramatic Strategies in the Plays of Edward Bond* (CUP, Cambridge, 1992)

S. Trussler, *New Theatre Voices of the Seventies* (Methuen, London, 1981: reprints 16 interviews from *Theatre Quarterly* 1970–80, including one with Bond, 'The Long Road to *Lear*', a shortened version of the next item.

Theatre Quarterly, Vol. II, No. 5, January–March 1972: contains two valuable items – 'The Long Road to *Lear*', an interview with Bond, and 'A Production Casebook of Bond's *Lear* at the Royal Court' based on notes made by Gaskill's assistant, G. Dark, containing comments by Gaskill and Bond as well as recording the stages of rehearsal and production.

Richard Findlater, *At the Royal Court: 25 Years of the English Stage Company* (Amber Lane Press, Ambergate, 1981): contains articles by dramatists, actors and directors connected with the Royal Court Theatre, including Ann Jellicoe on 'The Writers' Group' and Edward Bond on 'The Theatre I Want'.

Lear

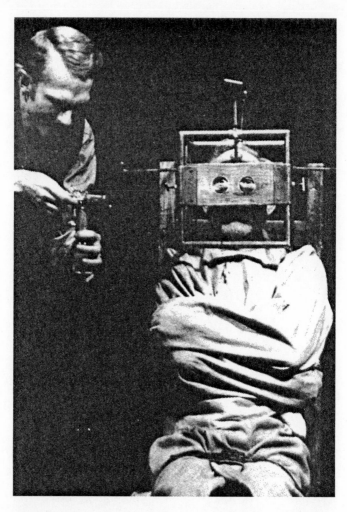

Lear and Fourth Prisoner (Act 2, Scene 6). Royal Court, 1971.

Author's Preface

I write about violence as naturally as Jane Austen wrote about manners. Violence shapes and obsesses our society, and if we do not stop being violent we have no future. People who do not want writers to write about violence want to stop them writing about us and our time. It would be immoral not to write about violence.

*

Many animals are able to be violent, but in non-human species the violence is finally controlled so that it does not threaten the species' existence. Then why is the existence of our species threatened by its violence?

I must begin with an important distinction. The predator hunting its prey is violent but not aggressive in the human way. It wants to eat, not destroy, and its violence is dangerous to the prey but not to the predator. Animals only become aggressive – that is destructive in the human sense – when their lives, territory or status in their group are threatened, or when they mate or are preparing to mate. Even then the aggression is controlled. Fighting is usually ritualized, and the weaker or badly-placed animal will be left alone when it runs away or formally submits. Men use much of their energy and skill to make more efficient weapons to destroy each other, but animals have often evolved in ways to ensure they *can't* destroy each other.

A lot has been written on this subject and it is not my job to repeat the evidence; but it shows clearly, I think, that in normal surroundings and conditions members of the same species are not dangerous to one another, but that when they are kept in adverse conditions, and forced to behave unnaturally, their behaviour deteriorates. This has been seen in zoos and laboratories. Then they become destructive and neurotic and make bad parents. They begin to behave like us.

That is all there is to our 'innate' aggression, or our 'original' sin as it was first called. There is no evidence of an aggressive *need*, as there is of sexual and feeding *needs*. We respond aggressively when we are constantly deprived of our physical and emotional needs, or when we are threatened with this; and if we are constantly deprived and threatened in this way – as human beings now are – we live in a constant state of aggression. It does not matter how much a man doing routine work in, say, a factory or office is paid: he will still be deprived in this sense. Because he is behaving in a way for which he is not designed, he is alienated from his natural self, and this will have physical and emotional consequences for him. He becomes nervous and tense and he begins to look for threats everywhere. This makes him belligerent and provocative; he becomes a threat to other people, and so his situation rapidly deteriorates.

This is all the facts justify us in concluding: aggression is an ability but not a necessity. The facts are often *interpreted* more pessimistically, but that is another matter.

If we *were* innately aggressive, in the sense that it was *necessary* for us to act aggressively from time to time, we would be condemned to live with an incurable disease; and as the suffering caused by aggression in a technological culture is so terrible, the question would arise: does the human race have any moral justification for its existence? A character in my play *Early Morning* answered no, and he tried to kill himself. It is astonishing that many people who share his beliefs are not forced to draw his conclusions, but can still go about their daily business. This ability shows mental shallowness and emotional glibness, not stoicism and spiritual strength. Their 'realism' is really only the fascism of lazy men.

Then why do we behave worse to one another than other animals? We live in ways for which we are not designed and so our daily existence interferes with our natural functioning, and this activates our natural response to threat: aggression. How has this happened? Why, in the first place, do we live in urban, crowded regimented groups, working like machines (mostly for the benefit of other men) and with no real control of our lives? Probably this situation could not have been avoided. Men did not suddenly become possessors of human minds and then use them to solve the problems of existence. These problems were constantly posed and solved within an inherited organization or social structure, and this structure was redeveloped to deal with new problems as they arose. So there was probably never much chance for new thinking. As men's minds clarified they were already living in herds or groups, and these would have evolved into tribes and societies. Like waking sleepers they would not know dream from reality.

What problems did these half-awake, superstitious men have to face? They were biologically so successful that they probably became too numerous for their environments and they could not go on living as loose bands of scavengers and hunters. And the environment itself changed, sometimes suddenly and sometimes gradually but inevitably. And perhaps the relationship between earlier instincts and human awareness produced its own problems. All these changes required adaptations in social organization and created new opportunities for leadership. Habits and techniques of control would be strengthened. In critical times any non-conformity would be a danger to the group. People who are controlled by others in this way soon lose the ability to act for themselves, even if their leaders do not make it dangerous for them to do so. And then, as I shall explain, the natural feelings of opposition become moralized and work to perpetuate the very organization they basically oppose. The whole structure becomes held together by the negative biological response to deprivation and threat – it is an organization held together by the aggression it creates. Aggression has become moralized, and morality has become a form of violence. I shall describe how this happens.

Once the social structure exists it tends to be perpetuated. The organizing groups, the leaders, receive privileges. Some of these were perhaps necessary in the critical situations that created the need for leadership. But the justification for them becomes less when they are inherited by their children. At the same time they become more extensive and entrenched. They become an injustice. But the organizing group becomes self-justifying, because although its position is unjust it is the administrator of justice. At first opposition to it will not be revolutionary or even political; it will be 'meaningless' and involve personal discontents and frustrations. When personal problems become private problems, as they must for the people involved in them, they are distorted, and then people seem to be acting in arbitrary, self-regarding ways. This can always be shown to be socially disruptive, of course. In this way an unjust society causes and defines crime; and an aggressive social structure which is unjust and must create aggressive social disruption, receives the moral sanction of being 'law and order'. Law and order is one of the steps taken to maintain injustice.

People with unjust social privileges have an obvious emotional interest in social morality. It allows them to maintain their privileges and justifies them in taking steps to do so. It reflects their fear of an opposition that would often take away everything they have, even their lives. This is one way in which social morality becomes angry and aggressive.

But there is another way. Social morality is also a safe form of

obedience for many of the victims of the unjust organization. It
gives them a form of innocence founded on fear – but it is never a
peaceful innocence. It is a sort of character easily developed in
childhood, when power relations are at their starkest. Then it is
dangerous to have aggressive ideas against those in power because
they can easily punish you, they are stronger and cleverer, and if
you destroyed them how could you live? (In adults this becomes:
We can't have a revolution because the buses wouldn't run and I'd
be late for work. Or: Hitler made the trains run on time.) Our
society has the structure of a pyramid of aggression and as the child
is the weakest member it is at the bottom. We still *think* we treat
children with special kindness and make special allowances for
them, as indeed most animals do. But do we? Don't most people
believe they have a right, even a duty, to use crude force against
children as part of their education? Almost all organizations dealing
with children are obsessed with discipline. Whenever possible we
put them into uniforms and examine their minds like warders
frisking prisoners. We force them to live by the clock before they
can read it, though this makes no biological sense. We build homes
without proper places for them. They interfere with the getting of
money so mothers leave them and go to work – and some of them
are no longer even physically able to feed their own children. Parents
are worn out by daily competitive striving so they can't tolerate the
child's natural noise and mess. They don't know why it cries, they
don't know *any* of its inarticulate language. The child's first word
isn't 'mummy' or 'daddy', it is 'me'. It has been learning to say it
through millions of years of evolution, and it has a biological right
to its egocentricity because that is the only way our species can
continue.

The point is this: every child is born with certain biological
expectations, or if you like species' assumptions – that it's un-
preparedness will be cared for, that it will be given not only food but
emotional reassurance, that its vulnerability will be shielded, that it
will be born into a world waiting to receive it, and that knows *how*
to receive it. But the weight of aggression in our society is so heavy
that the unthinkable happens: we batter it. And when the violence is
not so crude it is still there, spread thinly over years; the final effect
is the same and so the dramatic metaphor I used to describe it was
the stoning of a baby in its pram. This is not done by thugs but by
people who like plays condemning thugs.

One way or the other the child soon learns that it is born into a
strange world and not the world it evolved for: we are no longer

born free. So the small, infinitely vulnerable child panics – as any animal must. It does not get the reassurance it needs, and in its fear it identifies with the people who have power over it. That is, it accepts their view of the situation, their judgement of who is right and wrong – their *morality*. But this morality – which is social morality – now has all the force of the fear and panic that created it. Morality stops being something people want and becomes what they are terrified to be without. So social morality is a form of corrupted innocence, and it is against the basic wishes of those who have been moralized in this way. It is a threat, a weapon used against their most fundamental desire for justice, without which they are not able to be happy or allow others to be happy. The aggressive response of such people has been smothered by social morality, but this only increases its tension. So they try to relieve it in extravert ways. Often they become missionaries and campaigners. They are obsessed with a need for censorship – which is only the moral justification of the peeping Tom. They find the wicked and ungodly everywhere – because these things are in themselves. Their social morality denies their need for justice, but that need is so basic it can only be escaped by dying or going mad; otherwise it must be struggled against obsessively. In this struggle pleasure becomes guilt, and the moralizing, censorious, inhuman puritans are formed. Sometimes their aggression is hidden under strenuous gleefulness, but it is surprising how little glee is reflected in their opinions and beliefs, and how intolerant, destructive and angry these guardians of morality can be.

Their morality is angry because they are in conflict with themselves. Not merely divided, but *fighting* their own repressed need for justice with all the fear and hysteria of their original panic. Because this isn't something that is done once, in childhood or later; to go on living these people must murder themselves every day. Social morality is a form of suicide. Socially moralized people must act contemptuously and angrily to all liberalism, contentment and sexual freedom, because these are the things they are fighting in themselves. There is no way out for them – it is as if an animal was locked in a cage and then fed with the key. It shakes the bars but can never get out. So other people's happiness becomes their pain, and other people's freedom reminds them of their slavery. It is as if they had created in themselves a desolate, inhospitable landscape in which they had to live out their emotional and spiritual lives. This landscape reflects, of course, the inhospitable, unjust world in which they first suffered; and it exacerbates and reinforces their

aggression and seems to give it added depths of bitterness. By call-
ing the unjust world good they recreate it in themselves and are
condemned to live in it. They have not learned that when you are
frightened of the dark you do not make it go away by shutting your
eyes. These people are the angry, gleeful ghosts of my play, *Early
Morning*.

Not all children grow up in this way, of course. Some solve the
problem by becoming cynical and indifferent, others hide in a
listless, passive conformity, others become criminal and openly destructive. Whatever happens, most of them will grow up to act in ways
that are ugly, deceitful and violent; and the conforming, socially
moralized, good citizens will be the most violent of all, because
their aggression is expressed through all the technology and power
of massed society. The institutions of morality and order are always
more destructive than crime. This century has made that very clear.

Even if a child escapes undamaged it will still face the same
problems as a man. We treat men as children. They have no real
political or economic control of their lives, and this makes them
afraid of society and their own impotence in it. Marx has described
adult alienation very well, but we can now understand more about
it. We can see that most men are spending their lives doing things
for which they are not biologically designed. We are not designed
for our production lines, housing blocks, even cars; and these
things are not designed for us. They are designed, basically, to
make profit. And because we do not even need most of the things
we waste our lives in producing, we have to be surrounded by
commercial propaganda to make us buy them. This life is so
unnatural for us that, for straightforward biological reasons, we
become tense, nervous and aggressive, and these characteristics are
fed back into our young. Tension and aggression are even becoming
the markings of our species. Many people's faces are set in patterns
of alarm, coldness or threat; and they move jerkily and awkwardly,
not with the simplicity of free animals. These expressions are signs
of moral disease, but we are taught to admire them. They are used
in commercial propaganda and in iconographic pictures of politicians
and leaders, even writers; and of course they are taken as signs of
good manners in the young.

It is for these reasons I say that society is held together by the
aggression it creates, and men are not dangerously aggressive but
our sort of society is. It creates aggression in these ways: first, it is
basically unjust, and second it makes people live unnatural lives –
both things which create a natural, biological aggressive response in

the members of society. Society's formal answer to this is socialized morality; but this, as I have explained, is only another form of violence, and so it must itself provoke more aggression. There is no way out for our sort of society, an unjust society must be violent. Any organization which denies the basic need for biological justice must become aggressive, even though it claims to be moral. This is true of most religions, which say that justice can only be obtained in another world, and not in this. It is also true of many movements for political reform.

Moralized aggression can, of course, be mixed with ordinary kindness and decency, so can the aggression of the social institutions it maintains. But aggression is so powerful (it was after all evolved to deal with desperate situations) that it decides the character of all people and institutions it infects. So through historical times our institutions have been aggressive, and because of this they make it even easier for aggressive people to get power and authority. That is why leaders – revolutionary as well as reactionary – so often behave worse than animals. I don't say this as invective – it is a sad, historical truth.

So human aggression has important features that make it more destructive than the aggression of other animals. It *is* animal aggression, but it has to be accommodated by our human minds, and presumably it appears to us as more alarming and frightening than it does to other animals. This is true of our subjective feelings of aggression as well as of the aggression we meet from outside. We have more complicated resources to deal with this increased vulnerability. When panic and fear become unbearable it is as if we lied and said they were not there, and out of this lie we build social morality. Children are especially vulnerable in this way, as I have said, but we are all exposed to the same pressures throughout our lives. As animals we react to threat in a natural, biological way; but we must also react in more complicated ways as human beings – mentally, emotionally and morally. It is because we cannot do this successfully that we no longer function as a species. Instead we have created all the things that threaten us: our military giantism, moral hysteria, industrial servitude, and all the ugly aggressiveness of a commercial culture.

Our situation has been made much worse, at least for the time being, by our technological success. The problem can now be described in this brief, schematic way.

We evolved in a biosphere but we live in what is more and more becoming a technosphere. We do not fit into it very well and so it activates our biological defences, one of which is aggression. Our environment is changing so rapidly that we cannot wait for biological solutions to evolve. So we should either change our technosphere or use technology to change human nature. But change in our society is really decided on urgent commercial imperatives, so nothing is done to solve our main problem. But a species living in an unfavourable environment dies out. For us the end will probably be quicker because the aggression we generate will be massively expressed through our technology.

This is very over-simplified and our fate is far from being so certain. But the combination of technology and socialized morality is very ugly, and it could lead to disaster. Alternatively, governments could begin to use technology to enforce socialized morality. That is by using drugs, selection, conditioning, genetics and so on, they could manufacture people who would fit into society. This would be just as disastrous. So if we do not want either of these things we must do something else. There are signs, in the search for counter-cultures and alternative politics, that we are beginning to do so.

What ought we to do? Live justly. But what is justice? Justice is allowing people to live in the way for which they evolved. Human beings have an emotional and physical need to do so, it is their biological expectation. They *can* only live in this way, or all the time struggle consciously or unconsciously to do so. That is the essential thing I want to say because it means that in fact our society and its morality, which deny this, and its technology which more and more prevents it, all the time whisper into people's ear 'You have no right to live'. That is what lies under the splendour of the modern world. Equality, freedom and fraternity must be reinterpreted in the light of this – otherwise real revolutionary change is impossible.

We can express this basic need in many ways: aesthetic, intellectual, the need to love, create, protect and enjoy. These are not higher things that can be added when more basic needs are met. *They* are basic. They must be the way in which we express all our existence, and if they do not control our daily life then we cannot function as human beings at all. They are not weakness, but they have nothing to do with the caricatures that pass for strength in our society – the hysterical old maids who become sergeant majors, the disguised peeping Toms who become moralists, the immature social misfits who become judges. Society pays lip service to these needs, but it has no real interest in them, and they are of course incompatible with the strident competitiveness of a commercial culture. So really we deny them. Like ghosts we teach a dead religion, build a few more prisons to worship Caesar in, and leave it at that. Blake said that when we try to become more than men we become less than beasts, and that is what we have done. Our human emotions and intellects are not things that stand apart from the long development of evolution; it is as animals we make our highest demands, and in responding to them as men we create our deepest human experience.

I have not answered many of the questions I have raised, but I have tried to explain things that often go unnoticed but which must be put right if anything is to work for us. They are difficult to put right because reforms easily become socially moralized. It is so easy to subordinate justice to power, but when this happens power takes on the dynamics and dialectics of aggression, and then nothing is really changed. Marx did not know about this problem and Lenin discovered it when it was too late.

There is no need for pessimism or resignation, and this play is certainly not either of these things. Lear is blind till they take his eyes away, and by then he has begun to see, to understand. (Blindness is a dramatic metaphor for insight, that is why Gloucester, Oedipus and Tiresias are blind.) Lear's new world is strange and so at first he can only grope painfully and awkwardly. Lear is old by then, but most of the play's audiences will be younger. It might seem to them that the truth is always ground for pessimism when it is discovered, but one soon comes to see it as an opportunity. Then you don't have to go on doing things that never work in the hope that they might one day – because now you know why they *can't*. Even bourgeois politics is more efficient than that.

Finally, I have not tried to say what the future should be like, because that is a mistake. If your plan of the future is too rigid you start to coerce people to fit into it. We do not need a plan of the future, we need a *method* of change.

I want to say something brief about the play. Lear did not have to destroy his daughters' innocence, he does so only because he doesn't understand his situation. When he does understand he leaves Thomas and Susan unharmed. But I think he had to destroy the innocent boy. Some things were lost to us long ago as a species, but we all seem to have to live through part of the act of losing them. We have to learn to do this without guilt or rancour or callousness – or socialized morality. So Lear's ghost isn't one of the angry ghosts from *Early Morning*, but something different.

Apart from the ten or so main characters of the play there are about seventy other speaking parts. In a sense these are one role showing the character of a society.

Act One shows a world dominated by myth. Act Two shows the clash between myth and reality, between superstitious men and the autonomous world. Act Three shows a resolution of this, in the world we prove real by dying in it.

According to ancient chronicles Lear lived about the year 3100 after the creation. He was king for 60 years. He built Leicester and was buried under the River Soar. His father was killed while trying to fly over London. His youngest daughter killed herself when she fell from power.

(HOLINSHED and GEOFFREY OF MONMOUTH)

LEAR *was presented by the English Stage Company at the Royal Court Theatre on September 29th 1971 with the following cast:*

FOREMAN	Geoffrey Hinsliff
1ST WORKMAN	Matthew Guinness
2ND WORKMAN	Struan Rodger
3RD WORKMAN	Ron Pember
SOLDIER	Bob Hoskins
LEAR	Harry Andrews
BODICE	Carmel McSharry
FONTANELLE	Rosemary McHale
WARRINGTON	Anthony Douse
OLD COUNCILLOR	George Howe
ENGINEER	Gareth Hunt
FIRING SQUAD OFFICER	William Hoyland
BISHOP	Gareth Hunt
DUKE OF NORTH	Eric Allen
DUKE OF CORNWALL	Alec Heggie
SOLDIER A	Bob Hoskins
THE GRAVEDIGGER'S BOY	Mark McManus
THE GRAVEDIGGER'S BOY'S WIFE	Celestine Randall
CARPENTER	Oliver Cotton
SERGEANT	Bob Hoskins
SOLDIER D *at the Gravedigger's Boy's House*	Ray Barron
SOLDIER E *at the Gravedigger's Boy's House*	Geoffrey Hinsliff
SOLDIER F *at the Gravedigger's Boy's House*	Antony Milner
JUDGE	William Hoyland
USHER	Gareth Hunt
OLD SAILOR	Matthew Guinness

BEN, *a Prison Orderly*	Derek Carpenter
SOLDIER H *Guard in the Prison*	Geoffrey Hinsliff
SOLDIER I *Guard in the Prison*	Richard Howard
SOLDIER G *Guard in the Prison*	Bob Hoskins
OLD PRISON ORDERLY	Anthony Douse
WOUNDED REBEL SOLDIER	Matthew Guinness
BODICE'S AIDE (Major Pellet)	Struan Rodger
SOLDIER J *Convoy Escort*	Bob Hoskins
SOLDIER K *Convoy Escort*	Geoffrey Hinsliff
SOLDIER L *Convoy Escort*	Richard Howard
PRISONER 1	Struan Rodger
PRISONER 2	Ron Pember
PRISONER 3	Derek Carpenter
PRISONER 4, *later Prison Doctor*	William Hoyland
PRISON COMMANDANT	Gareth Hunt
SOLDIER M *Prison Guard*	Ray Barron
SOLDIER N *Prison Guard*	Matthew Guinness
SOLDIER O *Prison Guard*	Eric Allen
FARMER	Geoffrey Hinsliff
FARMER'S WIFE	Marjorie Yates
FARMER'S SON	Antony Milner
THOMAS	Alec Heggie
JOHN	Richard Howard
SUSAN	Diana Quick
SMALL MAN	Ron Pember
OFFICER	Gareth Hunt
A BOY	Ray Barron

OTHER SOLDIERS, WORKERS, STRANGERS, COURT OFFICIALS, GUARDS: Geoffrey Hinsliff, Matthew Guinness, Antony Milner, Ray Barron, Ron Pember, Eric Allen, Anthony Douse, Bob Hoskins, Richard Howard, Gareth Hunt, Derek Carpenter, Marjorie Yates, Struan Rodger.

Directed by William Gaskill   *Costumes designed by Deirdre Clancy*
Sets designed by John Napier   *Lighting by Andy Phillips*

Act One

SCENE ONE

Near the wall.
A stack of building materials – shovels, picks, posts and a tarpaulin.
Silence. Then (offstage) a sudden indistinct shout, a crash, shouts. A
FOREMAN *and* TWO WORKERS *carry on a* DEAD WORKER *and*
put him down. They are followed by a SOLDIER.

FIRST WORKER. Get some water! He needs water.
FOREMAN. He's dead.
SOLDIER. Move 'im then!
FOREMAN. Get his legs.
SOLDIER (*to* FOREMAN). Can yer see 'em? Look an' see! They're
  comin' up the ditch on the other side.

> FOREMAN *goes upstage to look off.* THIRD *and* FOURTH
> WORKERS *come on.*

THIRD WORKER (*coming on*). I shouted to him to run.
FOREMAN (*coming downstage*). Go back, go back! Work!

> FOURTH WORKER *goes off again.*

THIRD WORKER. You heard me shout!
FIRST WORKER. He says he's dead.
FOREMAN. Work!
SOLDIER (*to* FIRST WORKER). You! – make yerself responsible
  for 'andin' in 'is pick t' stores. (*Suddenly he sees something off*
  stage and runs down to the others.) Cover 'im! Quick!
FOREMAN (*points to tarpaulin*). Take that!

> *They cover the body with the tarpaulin.* LEAR, LORD
> WARRINGTON, *an* OLD COUNCILLOR, *an* OFFICER, *an*
> ENGINEER *and* LEAR'S DAUGHTERS – BODICE *and*

FONTANELLE – *come on. The* SOLDIER, FOREMAN *and* WORKERS *stand stiffly.* WARRINGTON *signs to them and they work by the tarpaulin.*

BODICE (*to* FONTANELLE). We needn't go on. We can see the end.

ENGINEER. The chalk ends here. We'll move faster now.

COUNCILLOR (*looking at his map*). Isn't it a swamp on this map?

FONTANELLE (*to* BODICE). My feet are wet.

LEAR (*points to tarpaulin*). What's that?

ENGINEER. Materials for the –

WARRINGTON (*to* FOREMAN). Who is it?

FOREMAN. Workman.

WARRINGTON. What?

FOREMAN. Accident, sir.

LEAR. Who left that wood in the mud?

ENGINEER. That's just delivered. We're moving that to –

LEAR. It's been rotting there for weeks. (*To* WARRINGTON.) They'll never finish! Get more men on it. The officers must make the men work!

BODICE (*shakes* ENGINEER's *hand*). Our visit has been so enjoyable and informative.

FONTANELLE. Such an interesting day.

WARRINGTON. We can't take more men. The countryside would be left derelict and there'd be starvation in the towns.

LEAR. Show me this body.

WARRINGTON *and the* SOLDIER *lift the tarpaulin.*

Blow on the head.

FOREMAN. Axe.

LEAR. What?

FOREMAN. An axe, sir. Fell on him.

LEAR. It's a flogging crime to delay work. (*To* WARRINGTON.) You must deal with this fever. They treat their men like cattle. When they finish work they must be kept in dry huts. All these huts are wet. You waste men.

COUNCILLOR (*making a note*). I'll appoint a hut inspector.

LEAR. They dug the wall up again last night.

OFFICER. Local farmers. We can't catch them, they scuttle back home so fast.

LEAR. Use spring traps. (*To* FOREMAN.) Who dropped the axe?

WARRINGTON (*to* FOREMAN). Be quick!

FOREMAN *and* SOLDIER *push* THIRD WORKER *forward*.

LEAR. Court martial him. Fetch a firing squad. A drumhead trial for sabotage.

Quiet murmur of surprise. The OFFICER *goes to fetch the* FIRING SQUAD.

FONTANELLE. My feet are wet.

BODICE. She'll catch cold, father.

LEAR. Who was a witness?

WARRINGTON (*points to* FOREMAN). You!

FOREMAN. He dropped a pickaxe on his head. I've had my eye on him, sir. Always idle and –

LEAR (*to* THIRD WORKER). Prisoner of war?

FOREMAN. No. One of our men. A farmer.

LEAR. I understand! He has a grudge. I took him off his land.

The FIRING SQUAD *is marched in by the* OFFICER.

OFFICER. Squad as a squad – halt!

LEAR. I shall give evidence. He killed a workman on the wall. That alone makes him a traitor. But there's something else suspicious about him. Did you dig up the wall last night?

BODICE (*sighing*). It can easily be checked if he missed their roll calls.

LEAR. I started this wall when I was young. I stopped my enemies in the field, but there were always more of them. How could we ever be free? So I built this wall to keep our enemies out. My people will live behind this wall when I'm dead. You may be governed by fools but you'll always live in peace. My wall will make you free. That's why the enemies on our borders – the Duke of Cornwall and the Duke of North – try to stop us building it. I won't ask him which he works for – they're both hand in glove. Have him shot.

THIRD WORKER. Sir.

FONTANELLE (*aside to* BODICE). Thank god we've thought of ourselves.

OFFICER. Squad as a squad to firing positions – move!

LEAR (*indicating the* FIRING SQUAD). They must work on the wall, they're slow enough. (*Turns to* WARRINGTON.) See this is done. I'm going down to the swamp.

BODICE. Father, if you kill this man it will be an injustice.

LEAR. My dear, you want to help me, but you must let me deal with the things I understand. Listen and learn.

BODICE. What is there to learn? It's silly to make so much out of nothing. There was an accident. That's all.

LEAR (*half aside to her*). Of course there was an accident. But the work's slow. I must do something to make the officers move. That's what I came for, otherwise my visit's wasted. And there *are* saboteurs and there *is* something suspicious about this man –

BODICE. But think of the people! They already say you act like a schoolboy or an old spinster –

LEAR. Why are they waiting? It's cruel to make him wait.

OFFICER ⎫ Sir – you're –
WARRINGTON ⎭ Move, sir.

LEAR *moves out of the* FIRING SQUAD's *way.*

BODICE (*loudly*). Listen to me. All of you notice I disassociate myself from this act.

LEAR. Be quiet, Bodice. You mustn't talk like that in front of me.

FONTANELLE. And I agree with what my sister says.

LEAR. O my poor children, you're too good for this world. (*To the others.*) You see how well they'll govern when I'm dead. Bodice, you're right to be kind and merciful, and when I'm dead you *can* be – because you will have my wall. You'll live inside a fortress. Only I'm not free to be kind or merciful. I must build the fortress.

BODICE. How petty it is to be obstinate over nothing.

LEAR. I have explained and now you must understand!

BODICE. It is small and petty to make –

LEAR. I have explained.

BODICE. Small and petty! All these things are in your head. The Duke of Cornwall is not a monster. The Duke of North has not sworn to destroy you. I have proof of what I say.

LEAR. They're my sworn enemies. I killed the fathers therefore the sons must hate me. And when I killed the fathers I stood on the field among our dead and swore to kill the sons! I'm too old now, they've fooled me. But they won't take my country and dig my bones up when I'm dead. Never.

FONTANELLE (to BODICE). This is the moment to tell him.

BODICE. I'm going to marry the Duke of North and my sister's going to marry the Duke of Cornwall.

FONTANELLE. He's good and reliable and honest, and I trust him as if we'd been brought up together.

BODICE. Good lord! – how can they be your friends if you treat them like enemies? That's why they threatened you: it was political necessity. Well, now that's all in the past! We've brought them into your family and you can pull this absurd wall down. There! (Slight laugh.) You don't have to make your people slaves to protect you from your sons-in-law.

LEAR. My sons-in-law?

FONTANELLE. Congratulate us, father, give us your blessing.

BODICE. I'm marrying North.

FONTANELLE. And I'm marrying Cornwall.

LEAR (points to THIRD WORKER). Tie him straight! He's falling!

BODICE. So now you don't have to shoot him. Our husbands could never allow you to, anyway.

FONTANELLE. I know you'll get on with my husband. He's very understanding, he knows how to deal with old people.

LEAR. Straighter!

BODICE. You'll soon learn to respect them like your sons.

LEAR. I have no sons! I have no daughters! (*Tries to be calmer.*) Tell me – (*Stops, bewildered.*) – you are marrying North and you are marrying –. No, no! They've deceived you. You haven't met them. When did you meet them? Behind my back?

FONTANELLE. We sent each other photographs and letters. I can tell a man from his expression.

LEAR. O now I understand! You haven't met them. You're like blind children. Can't you see they only want to get over the wall? They'll be like wolves in a fold.

BODICE. Wall, wall, wall! This wall must be pulled down!

FONTANELLE. Certainly. My husband insists on that as part of the marriage contract.

BODICE (*to* OFFICER). I order you not to shoot this man. Our husbands will shoot anyone who shoots him. They offer us peace, we can't shoot innocent men because we think they're their spies!

LEAR. Shoot him!

BODICE. No!

LEAR. This is not possible! I must be obeyed!

WARRINGTON. Sir, this is out of hand. Nothing's gained by being firm in little matters. Keep him under arrest. The Privy Council will meet. There are more important matters to discuss.

LEAR. My orders are not little matters! What duke are you marrying? Who have you sold me to?

BODICE. If the king will not act reasonably it's your legal duty to disobey him.

WARRINGTON. Ma'am, you make this worse. Let me –

LEAR (*takes pistol from the* OFFICER *and threatens the* FIRING SQUAD). Shoot him!

BODICE. There, it's happened. Well, the doctors warned us, of course. (*Loudly.*) My father isn't well. Warrington, take the king back to his camp.

FONTANELLE. He shouldn't have come out today. This mud's too much for him. My feet are wringing.

LEAR. My enemies will not destroy my work! I gave my life to
these people. I've seen armies on their hands and knees in
blood, insane women feeding dead children at their empty
breasts, dying men spitting blood at me with their last breath,
our brave young men in tears –. But I could bear all this! When
I'm dead my people will live in freedom and peace and remember my name, no – venerate it! . . . They are my sheep and if
one of them is lost I'd take fire to hell to bring him out. I loved
and cared for all my children, and now you've sold them to their
enemies! (*He shoots* THIRD WORKER, *and his body slumps forwards on the post in a low bow.*) There's no more time, it's too
late to learn anything.

BODICE. Yes, you'll ruin yourself. Our husbands can't let you
terrorize these people – they'll be *their* people soon. They must
protect them from your madness.

LEAR. Work! Get your men to work! Get them on the wall!

WORKERS, SOLDIERS *and* FOREMAN *go out. They take the
two bodies with them.*

I knew it would come to this! I knew you were malicious! I built
my wall against *you* as well as my other enemies! You talk of
marriage? You have murdered your family. There will be no
more children. Your husbands are impotent. That's not an
empty insult. You wrote? My spies know more than that! You
will get nothing from this crime. You have perverted lusts. They
won't be satisfied. It *is* perverted to want your pleasure where it
makes others suffer. I pity the men who share your beds. I've
watched you scheme and plan – they'll lie by you when you
dream! Where will your ambition end? You will throw old men
from their coffins, break children's legs, pull the hair from old
women's heads, make young men walk the streets in beggary
and cold while their wives grow empty and despair – I am
ashamed of my tears! You have done this to me. The people will
judge between you and me.

LEAR *goes out. The* ENGINEER *and the* OLD COUNCILLOR *follow him.*

WARRINGTON. I'm sorry, ma'am. If you'd spoken another time –
FONTANELLE. You should have taken him away when you were told –
BODICE. You were caught out. Well, learn your lesson. As it happens, no harm's done. Go and keep in with him. We'll let you know what must happen next.

WARRINGTON *and the others go out.* BODICE *and* FONTANELLE *are left alone.*

We must go to our husbands tonight.
FONTANELLE. Happiness at last! I was always terrified of him.
BODICE. We must attack before the wall's finished. I'll talk to my husband and you talk to yours. The four of us will sit in the Council of War. We must help each other. Goodbye.
FONTANELLE. Goodbye.

The daughters go out.

SCENE TWO

Parade ground.
A saluting stand. LEAR, OLD COUNCILLOR, WARRINGTON, BISHOP, MILITARY AIDES. *Marching, march music, and parade commands are heard during the scene.* LEAR *stands with both arms stretched out in a gesture of salute and blessing.*

LEAR. Greetings to the eighth regiment! (*Still saluting. To* WARRINGTON.) You will command my right flank and circle them on the right. Then I attack the centre. That's how I crushed the fathers. (*Still saluting.*) I salute my loyal comrades!
WARRINGTON. We could refuse this war. We're old, sir. We could retire and let these young men choose what to do with

their own lives. Ask your daughters to let you live quietly in the country.

LEAR (*still saluting*). How could I trust myself to them? My daughters are proclaimed outlaws, without rights of prisoners of war. They can be raped – or murdered. Why should they be held for trial? Their crimes aren't covered by my laws. Where does their vileness come from?

WARRINGTON. I've given you advice it was my duty to give. But I'm proud you've rejected it.

LEAR (*still saluting*). Greetings to my glorious ninth!

WARRINGTON. I have two letters from your daughters, sir. They both wrote in secret and told me not to let anyone know, especially each other.

LEAR. Give them to me.

WARRINGTON. No, sir. They ask me to betray you and then each other. They'll both make me head of the army and let me share their bed.

LEAR. They live in their own fantasies! They chose their husbands well, they should be married to my enemies! Have the war ceremonies taken place? It doesn't matter. (*He takes the letters from* WARRINGTON. *He reads part of one.*) 'He is mad. If he won what security would you have?' (*He reads from the other.*) 'He would turn on you as he turned on us.' (*Salutes as before.*) Greetings to my friends the ninth! (*Still saluting.*) Warrington, if I'm killed or fall into their hands you must take my place and build the wall.

WARRINGTON. Sir. This fry won't take you. Your army is paraded!

BISHOP. Our prayers go with you into war, sir. God blesses the righteous. He has nothing to do with women who make war.

COUNCILLOR. I feel confidence in my bones. That's never failed me. If only I were a young man!

LEAR. The trumpet! I smell victory!

Cheers and trumpet. They go out.

SCENE THREE

Daughters' War Council.
Table, chairs, map. BODICE, FONTANELLE, NORTH, CORNWALL.
BODICE *knits.*

NORTH. We share the command between us.

CORNWALL. Yes.

NORTH. We must guess how Lear will attack.

BODICE (*knitting*). He'll send Warrington round the right and attack the centre himself.

CORNWALL. Are you sure, sister?

BODICE. He always has and he's set in his ways.

> CORNWALL, NORTH *and* BODICE *study the map.* BODICE *knits at the same time.*

FONTANELLE (*aside*). I'm bitterly disappointed in my husband. How dare he! A civil servant wrote his letters and an actor posed for his photographs. When he gets on top of me I'm so angry I have to count to ten. That's long enough. Then I wait till he's asleep and work myself off. I'm not making do with that for long. I've written to Warrington and told him to use all his men against Bodice and leave my army alone – that'll finish her – and then I paid a young, blond lieutenant on my husband's staff to shoot him while they're busy fighting. Then I'll marry Warrington and let him run the country for me.

NORTH (*studying the map*). They can't get round these mountains.

CORNWALL. No.

BODICE (*aside*). I'm not disappointed in my husband. I expected nothing. There is some satisfaction in listening to him squeak on top of me while he tries to get his little paddle in. I lie still and tell myself while he whines, you'll pay for this, my lad. He sees me smiling and contented and thinks it's his virility. Virility! It'd be easier to get blood out of a stone, and far more probable. I've bribed a major on his staff to shoot him in the

battle – they're all corrupt – and I've written to Warrington and
told him to use all his force against hers. She'll be crushed and
then I'll marry Warrington and run the country through him.
So I shall have three countries: my father's, my husband's and
my sister and brother-in-law's.

NORTH. Till tomorrow.

CORNWALL. Yes. (*Goes to* FONTANELLE.) Let's go to bed. I need
your body before I risk death.

FONTANELLE. My darling. (*Aside.*) I'll get him drunk. He's such
a frightened little boy, fighting terrifies him. He'll fidget and
mawl all night. I'd rather mop up his vomit.

NORTH (*to* BODICE). Let me take you to bed, my dear. I must feel
you on me when I go to the field.

BODICE. Yes, North. (*Aside.*) He must prove himself a man before
he plays with his soldiers. He'll fuss and try all night, but he
won't be able to raise his standard. I'll help him and make it
worse. By the morning he won't know which side he's fighting
on. And that'll make it easier for the major.

FONTANELLE. Sleep well.

BODICE. And you.

They all go out.

SCENE FOUR

Prison area.
THREE SOLDIERS (A, B *and* C) *upstage.*

SOLDIER A. 'Ow long they goin' a keep us 'ere? The war's over.
They wan'a send us 'ome.

SOLDIER B. They'll think a some reason. (*Indicates offstage.*)
Watered 'im yet?

SOLDIER A. No point.

BODICE, FONTANELLE *and an* OFFICER *hurry on downstage.*

BODICE. Is our father taken yet?

OFFICER. He got away.

FONTANELLE (*stamps her foot*). Damn! That's spoiled everything!

  CORNWALL *comes on.*

  (*Aside.*) My husband! Damn! Damn! Damn! Has the lieutenant dared to betray me?

CORNWALL (*kisses* FONTANELLE). A great victory! They fought like devils but we beat them!

BODICE (*aside*). If I hadn't told him father's plans he'd be lying dead under his army by now.

  NORTH *comes in.*

  (*Aside.*) Damn it! My husband!

NORTH (*kisses* BODICE). Your enemies are routed!

FONTANELLE (*to* CORNWALL. *Prying*). What are our losses? Are your staff all safe?

NORTH. I lost one major. He was talking to one of Cornwall's lieutenants before the fighting –

CORNWALL. A young blond man called Crag.

FONTANELLE. Yes, I knew him.

CORNWALL. – the first shell fell between them and blew their heads off.

BODICE (*aside*). One can't allow for everything.

NORTH. Warrington's in the cage.

BODICE (*aside*). Now I must be careful. He didn't attack my sister's men, so I couldn't risk him talking about my letter. I had his tongue cut out.

CORNWALL. Let's go and see what he has to say for himself.

FONTANELLE. Wait . . . (NORTH and CORNWALL *stop.*) He was shouting insults about you and I didn't want our troops to be upset. So I let them cut his tongue out. I thought that was best.

CORNWALL. O, my men would have laughed at him.

BODICE (*aside*). I see my sister thinks like me, I must never trust her.

NORTH. It doesn't matter, he's going to be killed anyway.

BODICE. I'll see to that for you. Go and thank our armies. (*Aside.*) He could still make signs. It's better if he dies in silence.

NORTH. Yes, Cornwall, let's go together.

CORNWALL *and* NORTH *go out with the* OFFICER.

BODICE. I'm glad they've gone. Men are squeamish after a war. (*To* SOLDIER A.) Private, you look strong and capable, would you like to go up in the world?

SOLDIER A. Yessam.

FONTANELLE. Good teeth, too.

BODICE. Get rid of them.

SOLDIER A *flicks his head and* SOLDIERS B *and* C *go out.*

Fetch him out.

SOLDIER A *fetches* WARRINGTON *on stage. He is dishevelled, dirty and bound.*

SOLDIER A. Yer wan' 'im done in in a fancy way? Thass sometimes arst for. I once 'ad t' cut a throat for some ladies t' see once.

FONTANELLE. It's difficult to choose.

BODICE (*sits on her riding stick and takes out her knitting*). Let him choose. (*Knits.*)

SOLDIER A. I once give a 'and t' flay a man. I couldn't manage that on me own. Yer need two at least for that. Shall I beat 'im up?

FONTANELLE. You're all talk! Wind and piss!

SOLDIER A. Juss for a start. Don't get me wrong, thass juss for a start. Get it goin' and see 'ow it goes from there.

FONTANELLE. But I want something –

BODICE (*knitting*). O shut up and let him get on with it. (*Nods at* SOLDIER A *to go on.*)

SOLDIER A. Thankyermum. Right, less see 'ow long it takes t' turn yer inside out.

FONTANELLE. Literally?

SOLDIER A (*hits* WARRINGTON). O, 'e wants it the 'ard way.
(*Hits him.*) Look at 'im puttin' on the officer class! (*Hits him.*)
Don't pull yer pips on me, laddie.

FONTANELLE. Use the boot! (SOLDIER A *kicks him.*) Jump on
him! (*She pushes* SOLDIER A.) Jump on his head!

SOLDIER A. Lay off, lady, lay off! 'Oo's killin' 'im, me or you?

BODICE (*knits*). One plain, two pearl, one plain.

FONTANELLE. Throw him up and drop him. I want to hear him
drop.

SOLDIER A. Thass a bit 'eavy, yer need proper gear t' drop 'em –

FONTANELLE. Do something! Don't let him get away with it. O
Christ, why did I cut his tongue out? I want to hear him
scream!

SOLDIER A (*jerks* WARRINGTON's *head up*). Look at 'is eyes, Miss.
Thass boney-fidey sufferin'.

FONTANELLE. O yes, tears and blood. I wish my father was
here. I wish he could see him. Look at his hands! Look at
them going! What's he praying or clutching? Smash his
hands!

> SOLDIER A *and* FONTANELLE *jump on* WARRINGTON's
> *hands.*

Kill his hands! Kill his feet! Jump on it – all of it! He can't hit
us now. Look at his hands like boiling crabs! Kill it! Kill all of
it! Kill him inside! Make him dead! Father! Father! I want to
sit on his lungs!

BODICE (*knits*). Plain, pearl, plain. She was just the same at
school.

FONTANELLE. I've always wanted to sit on a man's lungs. Let me.
Give me his lungs.

BODICE (*to* SOLDIER A). Down on your knees.

SOLDIER A. Me?

BODICE. Down! (SOLDIER A *kneels.*) Beg for his life.

SOLDIER A (*confused*). 'Is? (*Aside.*) What a pair! – O spare 'im,
mum.

BODICE (*knits*). No.

SOLDIER A. If yer could see yer way to. 'E's a poor ol' gent, lonely ol' bugger.

BODICE. It can't be pearl? I think there's an error in this pattern book.

FONTANELLE. O let me sit on his lungs. Get them out for me.

BODICE. I shall refuse his pardon. That always gives me my deepest satisfaction. Hold him up.

SOLDIER A *sits* WARRINGTON *upright.*

FONTANELLE. Look at his mouth! He wants to say something. I'd die to listen. O why did I cut his tongue out?

SOLDIER A. 'E's wonderin' what comes next. Yer can tell from 'is eyes.

BODICE (*pulls the needles from her knitting and hands the knitting to* FONTANELLE). Hold that and be careful.

SOLDIER A. Look at 'is eyes!

BODICE. It's my duty to inform you –

SOLDIER A. Keep still! Keep yer eyes on madam when she talks t'yer.

BODICE. – that your pardon has been refused. He can't talk or write, but he's cunning – he'll find some way of telling his lies. We must shut him up inside himself. (*She pokes the needles into* WARRINGTON's *ears.*) I'll just jog these in and out a little. Doodee, doodee, doodee, doo.

FONTANELLE. He can see my face but he can't hear me laugh!

BODICE. Fancy! Like staring into a silent storm.

FONTANELLE. And now his eyes.

BODICE. No . . . I think not. (*To* SOLDIER A.) Take him out in a truck and let him loose. Let people know what happens when you try to help my father. (*To* FONTANELLE.) Let me sit on his lungs! You old vulture! Go and flap round the battlefield.

FONTANELLE. Don't make fun of me. You're so stupid. You don't understand anything.

BODICE. I don't think I'd like to understand you. (*Takes her*

knitting from FONTANELLE.) You've let my knitting run!
(*Starts to go.*) Come on, we've won the war but we can't dilly-
dally, there's still part of the day left. I must see what my
husband's up to.

> BODICE *and* FONTANELLE *go out.* SOLDIER A *starts to take*
> WARRINGTON *out.*

SOLDIER A. It's all over. Walking offal! Don't blame me, I've got
a job t' do. If we was fightin' again t'morra I could end up
envyin' you anytime. Come on then, less 'ave yer. Yer'll live if
yer want to.

> *They go out.*

SCENE FIVE

Woods.
*A large empty plate and jug on the bare stage. Further down, a piece
of bread.* LEAR *and the* OLD COUNCILLOR *come in. They are
ragged, tired, dirty and frightened.*

COUNCILLOR. I've studied people, sir. Your daughters aren't
bad. Put yourself in their hands. They'll respond to your trust.
LEAR. Never. (*Stops.*) A jug and a plate. Empty!
COUNCILLOR. At least there are people about! I thought this was
the end of the world. Wait here, sir, and I'll look.
LEAR. No, don't leave me!
COUNCILLOR. There might be a village and I can get some food.
I'll be careful, sir. Sit down and rest.

> OLD COUNCILLOR *goes out.* LEAR *finds the bread on the
> ground.*

LEAR. Bread! Someone was eating this and they dropped it and
ran away. (*He eats it.*) That's all there is.

> LEAR *sits down. He is very tired.* WARRINGTON *comes on
> upstage. He is crippled and his face looks as if it's covered with*

bad plastic surgery. He carries a knife awkwardly. He's already seen LEAR *and comes on creeping towards him from behind.*

My daughters have taken the bread from my stomach. They grind it with my tears and the cries of famished children – and eat. The night is a black cloth on their table and the stars are crumbs, and I am a famished dog that sits on the earth and howls. I open my mouth and they place an old coin on my tongue. They lock the door of my coffin and tell me to die. My blood seeps out and they write in it with a finger. I'm old and too weak to climb out of this grave again.

WARRINGTON *sees someone coming and goes out.*

(*Looking off.*) Is this one of my daughters' men?

The GRAVEDIGGER'S BOY *comes on. He carries bread and water.*

No, there's no blood on him. – Who are you?
BOY. I live near here.
LEAR. Is that bread?
BOY. Yes.
LEAR. Is it poisoned?
BOY. No.
LEAR. Then my daughters didn't send him. They'd never miss a chance to poison good bread. Who's it for?
BOY. There's a man who roams round here. He's wild. They say he was wounded in the war.
LEAR. I'm hungry. I know you have no pity to sell, there's always a shortage of that in wartime, but you could sell me some bread. I can pay. (*Looks round.*) My friend keeps my money.
BOY. Take it. It's not much. (LEAR *eats.*) Have you come far?
LEAR. No.
BOY. Where are you going?
LEAR. I shan't know till I get there.
BOY. Was that your friend with the stick? He's left you, he wanted a horse to take him to town.

LEAR. The traitor! Give him a bad horse and let him break his neck!

BOY. I can't leave you out here on your own. I think you'd better come to my place for the night. Then you can think what to do.

LEAR. Your place? Have you any daughters?

BOY. No.

LEAR. Then I'll come. No daughters! Where he lives the rain can't be wet or the wind cold, and the holes cry out when you're going to tread in them.

The BOY *leads* LEAR *out.*

SCENE SIX

The GRAVEDIGGER'S BOY's *house.*
Wooden house upstage. A few steps to the front door. A well. A bench with bedding on it.
LEAR *and the* BOY *are sitting on the ground.*

BOY. My father was the village gravedigger. I liked to help him when I was a boy, and he taught me the work. He didn't want to be buried in a graveyard – you wouldn't want to be buried where you work.

The BOY'S WIFE *comes from the house with three bowls of soup. She gives the bowls out and sits by the* BOY. *The three eat.*

So when he died I found this place and started to dig his grave. And when I got down I struck a well. I thought, there's water here and some land, why do I want to dig graves all my life? So I live here and built this farm. (*Nods at bowl.*) It's good.

LEAR (*eating. To himself. The* BOY's WIFE *stares at him*). The mouse comes out of his hole and stares. The giant wants to eat the dragon, but the dragon has grabbed the carving knife.

BOY. My wife keeps pigs. I've got two fields and I catch things. No one minds out here. Any more?

LEAR *shakes his head. The* WIFE *takes the bowls inside.*

Now the nights are hot we've started to sleep outside. You can sleep inside if you like.

LEAR. I can't sleep on my own since I lost my army.

BOY. Then sleep out here. (*Indicates well.*) The well went dry in the summer. I had to dig down again. But it's all right now, I'm down to the spring.

LEAR (*to himself*). My daughters turned a dog out of its kennel because it got fond of its sack.

BOY. The pigs don't cost anything, I let them grub round all day and lock them up at night. They fatten themselves and I just have to slaughter them. Would you like a walk? I'll show you where we keep them. And then we must get to bed. I'm up early in the mornings. (*They stand. He calls into the house.*) Won't be long. Can you fetch the spare blanket? (*To* LEAR.) Take my arm.

LEAR. No. I once knew a man who was drowned on a bridge in a flood.

> LEAR *and the* BOY *go out. After a moment* WARRINGTON *comes on, still holding the knife. He has been watching* LEAR *and he now stares after him. He sees a movement through the doorway and hides. The* WIFE *comes out of the house with a blanket. She cries quietly, persistently and evenly, as if out of habit. She sees* WARRINGTON.

WIFE. Go away! (*She throws the blanket at him.*) Beggars, scroungers, filthy old men!

> *She looks round for something to throw. She runs into the house, crying loudly.* WARRINGTON *looks round in terror. He hides down the well. The* WIFE *comes out of the house with a soup bowl ready to throw. She can't see* WARRINGTON. *She sits down and cries loudly and bitterly.*
> *The* BOY *runs in.*

BOY. What is it? Are you all right?

WIFE (*crying*). Your wild man was here!

BOY. What did he do? Are you all right?

LEAR *walks in.*

LEAR. There's no one here.

WIFE (*crying*). Of course not! He ran away.

BOY. Don't cry.

WIFE (*crying*). I'm trying to stop.

BOY. He only wanted his food. I'll go up and feed him in the morning. Look, come and lie down. You're shivering. (*He spreads the blanket and pillow for her.*) Let me cover you up.

She lies down. She cries more quietly.

That's better. (*To* LEAR.) It's because she's carrying.

LEAR. Poor woman.

BOY (*taking* LEAR *to the other side of the stage*). We'd all better go to sleep, we don't want to disturb her. You can sleep here. (*He spreads a blanket and pillow.*) You'll be fine here. Good night.

BOY *goes back to his* WIFE *and lies beside her.* LEAR *sits on his blanket.*

LEAR (*to himself*). It is night. My daughters empty their prisons and feed the men to the dead in their graveyards. The wolf crawls away in terror and hides with the rats. Hup, prince! Hup rebel! Do tricks for human flesh! When the dead have eaten they go home to their pits and sleep. (*He lies down in an awkward pose and sleeps.*)

WIFE (*crying*). Hold me. Stop me crying.

BOY (*holding her*). You must take things easy now. You work too hard.

WIFE. Don't say that! It's not true!

BOY. All right, I won't.

WIFE. But you don't believe me.

BOY. Yes I do.

WIFE. You don't. I can see you don't. Why can't I make you happy?

BOY. I am happy.

WIFE. You're not. I know you're not. You make me happy – my father said I'd be unhappy here, but I'm not, you've made me so happy – why can't I make you happy? Look at the way you brought that man here! The first one you find! Why? I'm so afraid something will happen.

BOY. Does he matter to you?

WIFE. Of course he matters! And he's a tramp!

BOY. I'll make him wash.

WIFE. You see! You don't understand! Who is he?

BOY. I don't know. He told me he was an officer, but that's not true. Who'd take their orders from him!

WIFE. And he talks to himself. I'm afraid of him.

BOY. That's only a habit. He's lonely. You'll be all right, I thought you'd like someone to help you. He can look after the pigs.

WIFE. I knew it! You're going to ask him to stay!

BOY. What else can I do? He can't look after himself. He's a poor old man – how can I throw him out? Who'd look after him then? I won't do it!

WIFE. O you're a fool! Can anyone come who likes? Don't you have any sense of responsibility?

BOY. Responsibility!

LEAR. . . . When he saluted I saw blood on his hand . . .

WIFE. Listen!

LEAR. . . . I slept in the morning because all the birds were dead . . .

WIFE. . . . He's stopped.

BOY. O go to sleep. Please. For the child's sake.

Silence. They all sleep. WARRINGTON *comes out of the well. He still carries the knife. He goes to the* BOY *and his* WIFE *and peers down to see who they are. He crosses to* LEAR *and stops.*

Peers. Throws himself on LEAR, *roars, and hits him with the knife.* LEAR *jumps up.*

LEAR (*still dreaming*). My daughters – help me! There! Guards! (*Grabs* WARRINGTON *and stares at his face.*) What's this? . . . No! No!

The BOY *runs to* LEAR *and* WARRINGTON *runs out.*

A ghost!

BOY. He's gone! He ran!

LEAR. A ghost!

WIFE. It's the wild man! I saw him!

BOY. A light! (*The* WIFE *runs into the house.*) He's bleeding! Water! Cloth! (*To* LEAR.) Your arm! It's cut.

LEAR. He's dead! I saw his face! It was like a stone! I shall die!

The WIFE *comes out with a light.*

BOY. Water –

WIFE. Bring him inside! It's not safe out here!

BOY (*helping* LEAR *into the house*). Yes. Fetch the blanket. Quick. He's bleeding.

LEAR. I'll die! I've seen a ghost. I'm going to die. That's why he came back. I'll die.

BOY. The steps.

BOY *takes* LEAR *into the house. His* WIFE *picks up the blankets and follows them in.*

SCENE SEVEN

Same.
The next afternoon. There is no one there. The BOY *comes in. Takes off his hat and hangs it up on the side of the house. His* WIFE *comes in from the opposite side. She carries a pig pole and an empty swill bucket.*

WIFE. Is he still asleep?

BOY. I don't know. I just got back.

WIFE. You haven't asked him about last night.

BOY. Not yet. (*He kisses her.*) You're better.

WIFE. Yes. (*She takes the pole and bucket to the side of the house.*)
   The well's dirty, I saw it this morning when I did the washing.

BOY. O lord! I'll go down later on.

> *The* CARPENTER *comes in. He is tall and dark and carries a
> wooden box.*

Hello.

CARPENTER. Hello.

BOY. How are you?

CARPENTER. Fine. A bit busy.

BOY (*points to box*). What is it?

CARPENTER. Something I made.

BOY. It's early, but I'll go and shut the pigs up.

> *The* BOY *goes out.*

WIFE. What is it?

CARPENTER. A cradle. (*He gives it to her.*)

WIFE. O.

CARPENTER. He doesn't mind.

WIFE. It's beautiful.

> *The* CARPENTER *sits and looks at her. Slight pause.*

He's got someone staying here. An old man. You haven't seen
   him in the village?

CARPENTER. No. Who is he? I'll try and find out.

WIFE. He just brought him here to look after the pigs. Why? It's
   so silly, so silly . . .

CARPENTER (*after another slight pause*). Any jobs I can do?

WIFE. The door wants mending, but he'll do that.

CARPENTER. No, I left my tools in the cart down on the road. I'll
   fix it.

BOY (*off*). I-yoo! I-yoo! I-yoo! (*Two or three pigs squeal.*)

  LEAR *comes out of the house.*

LEAR (*puzzled*). I've slept all day. It's evening. (*Sees* CARPENTER.)
  Who's that?

WIFE. A man from the village.

LEAR. O. (*He sits on the cradle.*)

CARPENTER. ⎫ Not on that!
WIFE.   ⎭ You'll break it!

LEAR (*stands*). Where's your husband?

WIFE. He'll be here. I suppose you'll go away now after last night.

LEAR (*confused*). I don't know. I dreamed –

  The BOY *comes in.*

BOY. How are you? I thought I heard you up. Let me see your
  arm.

WIFE. John brought this.

BOY (*looks at the cradle*). O that's very clever. For the child.
  Thanks. (*The* CARPENTER *stands.*) You needn't go.

CARPENTER. Your wife wants me to fix her door.

  The CARPENTER *goes out. The* BOY *looks at* LEAR's *cut.*

WIFE (*picking up the cradle*). It's not deep.

BOY. It needs washing.

  The WIFE *goes into the house with the cradle.*

LEAR. Who is he?

BOY. Village carpenter. He makes coffins and cradles and mends
  chairs, anything. He's very good. Don't worry about him, he's
  always hanging round. He's in love with my wife.

LEAR. Last night I saw a ghost.

BOY (*amused*). My father said there aren't any, and he should
  know. It was this wild man.

LEAR. I see, I see . . . then it was all in my dream. (*Slight pause.*) I
  should have spent my life here.

BOY (*looking at the cut*). I'm sorry about this.

LEAR (*still confused and puzzled*). I've been cut before. It's almost gone. I was worse when I came here. You've looked after me well. I slept like a child in this silence all day. It's so long since I slept like that, I'd forgotten ... And now I shall get well again. It's so simple and easy here. (*Becoming angry.*) But where shall I go now, how can I live, what will become of me?

BOY. Stay here. You can look after my pigs. I can't pay you but you can eat and sleep with us.

LEAR. No. I'd get you into trouble. No, no. I must go away.

BOY. Listen, how many men were you in charge of?

LEAR. A few.

BOY. Well they won't come all this way for one old man who was in charge of a few other men. So stay.

LEAR. I could have a new life here. I could forget all the things that frighten me – the years I've wasted, my enemies, my anger, my mistakes. I've been too trusting, too lenient! I'm tormented by regrets – I must forget it all, throw it away! Yes! – let me live here and work for you.

BOY. Good. You'll be a real help to me when you've settled in. I'll be able to clear some more fields. You needn't worry about the soldiers. They're too busy looking for the king to worry about you. Did you know they're pulling his wall down?

LEAR. The wall?

BOY. Up and down, up and down. The king was mad. He took all the men from this village. But I hid. They'd worked with their hands all their lives but when they started on the wall their hands bled for a week.

LEAR. No.

BOY. You died of work or they shot you for not working. There was a disease –

LEAR. They tried to stop that.

BOY. – 'Wall death'. Their feet used to swell with the mud. The stink of it even when you were asleep! Living in a grave! He should come here – I'd go back to my old job and dig a grave for him! We used to dig his wall up at nights, when they were

working near here. (*Sighs.*) Let's talk about something else.
(LEAR *stops listening to him.*) My wife will be all right. She'll be
a bit cold at first, but she'll soon be glad to have you helping
us ... We're supposed to be a bad match. I know her father
didn't want us to marry. He's never come to see us. I asked him.
I don't like that, it makes you feel bad. He's a priest, he taught
her everything. She's very clever, but she can't understand
how I live. I've got my house, my farm, my wife – and every
night I tell her I love her. How could I be unhappy? She's
afraid it will change, she'd like to put a fence round us and shut
everyone else out.

His WIFE *comes out of the house with a long rope. She fixes it
across the back of the stage as a long clothes line. Short silence.*

LEAR. I remember some of my dream. There was a king and he
had a fountain in his garden. It was as big as the sea. One night
the fountain howled and in the morning the king went to look
at it. It was red. The servants emptied it and under the sea they
found a desert. The king looked in the sand and there was a
helmet and sword.

The WIFE *goes into the house.*

So the king –
BOY. I know that. A clown told it to us at the fair.

LEAR *stares at him. The* WIFE *comes out of the house with a
basket of washing.*

WIFE. I want some more water but it's dirty.
BOY (*stands*). I'll go down.

The WIFE *takes some pegs from the wall and starts to peg out a
line of white sheets. The* BOY *climbs into the well and goes out of
sight.*

LEAR (*to* WIFE). I'll do that. You mustn't work too hard.

She doesn't answer, but LEAR *helps her. They hang the sheets so that the bottoms just clear the ground.*

WIFE (*pegging*). Who is the wild man? You recognized him last night.

LEAR (*holding up a sheet*). No. I was dreaming.

WIFE (*taking the sheet*). When are you going?

LEAR (*picking up pegs*). Your husband's asked me to work for him.

WIFE (*pegging*). You're not stopping here. I won't have you.

LEAR (*handing her pegs*). He needs me. He said so.

WIFE (*taking the pegs*). I'm not having any dirty old tramps about. I'm carrying. I mustn't let myself get upset.

LEAR (*adjusting a sheet. Becoming angry*). You don't hang them straight.

WIFE (*pegging*). I could easily make him send you away.

LEAR. Straight.

WIFE (*pegging*). I don't want to have to do that. I'm not arguing and shouting any more, it upsets him too much. Please go – and don't tell him I made you.

LEAR (*holding up a sheet*). Where can I go?

WIFE (*taking the sheet*). Anywhere. You're free. You've got the whole world.

LEAR. He asked me to stay! No, I won't go! (*He crosses to the well.*) He said I could stay. He won't break his word. I'm too old to look after myself. I can't live in ditches and barns and beg for scraps and hire myself to peasants! No, I won't be at everyone's call! My daughters sent you! *You* go! It's you who're destroying this place! We must get rid of you! – (*He stops short and stares at the bucket.*)

WIFE. What is it?

LEAR. Blood.

WIFE. What?

LEAR. Blood. That's blood in the water. I've seen it before. (*Calls down the well.*) What are you doing? Where are you?

BOY (*off*). What?

WIFE. That's where he was hiding! (*Calls down well*.) He hid
down there last night – (*To* LEAR.) – and then he came up and
tried to kill you and ran away!

LEAR (*afraid*). No. There's too much blood . . . He came back and
he's down there now . . .

> *Silence. A* SERGEANT *and* THREE SOLDIERS (D, E *and* F)
> *come on. They all carry rifles.*

SOLDIER D. Don't run. I don't like breakin' women's legs.

SERGEANT. Turn it over inside.

> SOLDIERS D *and* E *go into the house.*

'Oo else yer got knockin' around?

LEAR. No one. You want me. We can go now.

> *He starts to go.* SOLDIER F *stops him.*

No, no! We must go.

SOLDIER F. 'Oo else? Shouldn't lie your age, time yer knowd
better.

SERGEANT. Come on, darlin', yer must a 'ad some one t' put yer
in that class.

SOLDIER F. Couldn't a bin 'im.

> SOLDIER D *comes out of the house.*

SOLDIER D. 'E'd 'ave t' use a carrot.

SOLDIER F. 'E would, the dirty ol' toe rag.

WIFE. Go away –

SOLDIER D (*to* SERGEANT). Empty.

WIFE. – he's gone.

SERGEANT. 'Oo'd leave a nice little lay like you?

> SOLDIER E *comes from behind the house.*

SOLDIER E. Pigs out the back.

LEAR. I look after them!

SERGEANT. We know there's a young fella.

LEAR. There's no one else. Take me away.

BOY (*off*). He's here! I've got him!

The SOLDIERS *stare. They are puzzled.*

LEAR. We can go. The girl didn't know who I am. I'll report you
for –

SOLDIER F *puts his hand over* LEAR's *mouth. Silence.*

BOY (*off*). His neck's broken.

SOLDIER D *points to the well.*

SERGEANT (*threatens* LEAR *with his rifle*). Tell 'im somethin'.

LEAR (*speaking down the well*). Yes.

BOY (*off*). He's dead. I'll bring him up. Pull the rope.

The SERGEANT *pulls the rope. The* SOLDIERS *take the* WIFE
and hide behind the sheets with her.

(*Off. Nearer.*) Steady.

LEAR goes upstage, sits on the steps or the bench and watches. The
SERGEANT goes behind the sheets. The BOY *comes out of the well,*
carrying WARRINGTON. WARRINGTON *is dripping wet.*

He fell down. He must have died straight away. My God! –
he's breathing. There's bubbles on his mouth! Look! Help me!

He puts WARRINGTON *down. A pool forms round him. The*
BOY *looks at* LEAR. *Stops. Suddenly he panics and shouts.*

Cordelia! .

The SERGEANT *and* SOLDIERS E *and* F *come from behind the*
sheets.

Cordelia!

SOLDIER E *shoots him. He staggers upstage towards the sheets.*
His head is down. He clutches a sheet and pulls it from the line.
CORDELIA *stands behind it. Her head is down and she covers*

*her face with her hands. SOLDIER D is preparing to rape her.
The BOY turns slowly away and as he does so the sheet folds
round him. For a second he stands in silence with the white sheet
draped round him. Only his head is seen. It is pushed back in
shock and his eyes and mouth are open. He stands rigid. Suddenly a huge red stain spreads on the sheet.*

SERGEANT. Kill the pigs.

SOLDIER E *runs off.*

SOLDIER F (*peering down at* WARRINGTON). Chriss look at this!
SERGEANT (*to* SOLDIER D). Do that inside.
LEAR. She's pregnant.
SOLDIER D. It can play with the end.
SOLDIER F (*poking* WARRINGTON's *mouth with the end of his
rifle*). Look at this blowin' bubbles!

Off, squealing starts as the pigs are slaughtered. SOLDIER D
takes the WIFE *into the house. The* BOY *suddenly drops dead.*

SERGEANT. Drop 'im down the 'ole.

The SERGEANT *and* SOLDIER F *drop* WARRINGTON *down the
well.*

SOLDIER F. 'Ere's another one.
SERGEANT. Up!

They drop the BOY *down the well. He points to* LEAR.

An' run 'im down t' the truck.

The SERGEANT *goes into the house.*

SOLDIER F. Some jammy bastards 'ave all the fun. I don't fancy
old grandads.

Off, the pig squealing stops.

LEAR (*stands*). O burn the house! You've murdered the husband,
slaughtered the cattle, poisoned the well, raped the mother,

killed the child – you must burn the house! You're soldiers –
you must do your duty! My daughters expect it! O burn the
house! Burn the house! Burn the house!

SOLDIER F. Shut it an' move.

> SOLDIER F *takes* LEAR *outside.* SOLDIER E *comes on from
> behind the house.*

LEAR (*going*). O burn it down! Burn it!

> *There is blood on* SOLDIER E's *face, neck, hands, clothes and
> boots. In the house* CORDELIA *gives a high, short gasp.*

SOLDIER E (*muttering contentedly*). An' I'll 'ave 'er reekin' a pig
blood. Somethin' t' write 'ome t' tell mother.

> *The* CARPENTER *follows him on. He carries his tool pack. He
> takes a cold chisel from it.*

(*Sees* CARPENTER.) Yes? (*A fraction later he calls towards the
house.*) Sarge!

> *The* CARPENTER *kills him with a blow from the cold chisel.*

CARPENTER (*looks towards the house*). Are there more of you?

> *The* CARPENTER *picks up* SOLDIER D's *rifle and goes into the
> house. Slight pause. Three rifle shots from inside the house.
> Silence.*

Act Two

SCENE ONE

Courtroom.

NORTH *and* CORNWALL *enter and talk quietly together while the court assembles. There is a* JUDGE, USHER, CLERK *and other Officials.*

CORNWALL. Our wives will condemn him and have his life.

NORTH. Yes.

CORNWALL. I don't think we should let them have their way in too many things.

NORTH. Bodice is a good woman. But she's had to bear her troubles on her own too long. Perhaps it's too late for her to trust anyone.

CORNWALL. That's true of both of them. We'll put him in a safe prison. He'll die without us.

BODICE *and* FONTANELLE *come on. The* JUDGE *goes to them.*

BODICE. You've studied your instructions?

JUDGE. Indeed, ma'am.

BODICE. This is a political trial: politics is the higher form of justice. The old king's mad and it's dangerous to let him live. Family sentiment doesn't cloud our judgement. I've arranged to call the people who upset him most.

FONTANELLE. I'm a witness.

BODICE. Let him rattle on and condemn himself. Goad him if it helps – but not too openly.

JUDGE. I understand ma'am.

The JUDGE *takes his place.* LEAR *is brought in under guard.*

BODICE (*to* FONTANELLE). He's deteriorated. I must put the
  gaoler on the Honours List.

JUDGE. You are the late king?

LEAR. You know who I am. I gave you your job.

JUDGE. And these ladies are your daughters.

LEAR. No.

JUDGE. They are your daughters.

LEAR. No.

JUDGE. Don't you recognize them?

LEAR. I've never seen them.

JUDGE. Sit. (LEAR *sits*.) The late king says his daughters –

LEAR. They're not my daughters!

> BODICE *pushes* FONTANELLE. FONTANELLE *goes to the*
> *witness stand.*

FONTANELLE. I will tell the truth.

JUDGE. Ma'am, try to make the late king remember you.

FONTANELLE. Father, once you found a white horse on a battlefield. You gave it to me and it broke its leg on the ice. They tied
  it to a tree and shot it. Poor little Fontanelle cried.

LEAR. Poor horse.

FONTANELLE. Another time I asked you how high the wall would
  be. You held me over your head and said you still couldn't see
  over the top.

LEAR. I was always exact. – Take me back to my prison. We are
  freer there.

> FONTANELLE *shrugs and goes back to her seat beside* BODICE.
> BODICE *smiles at her. An* OLD SAILOR *is led to the witness*
> *stand.*

OLD SAILOR. I will tell the truth. I can't see. I was a sailor and the
  sea blinded me. I have a little sight, but in a mist. I showed you
  how to sail. Your voice hasn't changed. You came back when
  you were king and showed me your daughters. I could see in
  those days. These are your daughters, sir.

LEAR. Are you taken care of?

OLD SAILOR. I've been blind seven years, sir. They say I have clear eyes, but they don't see for me.

LEAR. Are you well looked after, sir?

OLD SAILOR. Yes, sir. I have a good daughter.

LEAR. Go home and watch her. They change faster than the wind at sea.

The OLD SAILOR *is led away. The* OLD COUNCILLOR *goes to the witness stand.*

COUNCILLOR. I will tell the truth. (*Takes out his notebook.*) Sir, you know me.

LEAR. Through and through.

COUNCILLOR (*looks in notebook*). I helped you to escape on –

LEAR. You ran after me to be saved.

COUNCILLOR. Now you shouldn't say –

LEAR. And when you saw that I was finished you ran back here.

COUNCILLOR. I did my duty as a man of conscience –

LEAR. Convenience!

COUNCILLOR. Sir, when I saw that –

LEAR. I would be caught –

COUNCILLOR. – you were mentally disturbed –

LEAR. – you betrayed me! Is there no honour between old men? You've been corrupted by your children!

BODICE. Give him my mirror! (*Aside to* JUDGE.) Madmen are frightened of themselves!

The USHER *goes towards her but* BODICE *walks past him and takes the mirror to* LEAR.

LEAR. How ugly that voice is! That's not my daughter's voice. It sounds like chains on a prison wall. (BODICE *puts the mirror in his hand and walks back to her chair*.) And she walks like something struggling in a sack. (LEAR *glances down briefly at the mirror*.) No, that's not the king.

JUDGE. Take the oath first.

LEAR. You have no right to sit there!

JUDGE. Take the oath.

LEAR. I gave you your job because you were corrupt!

JUDGE. Take the oath.

LEAR. The king is always on oath! (*He stares down at the mirror.*) No, that's not the king . . . This is a little cage of bars with an animal in it. (*Peers closer.*) No, no, that's not the king! (*Suddenly gestures violently. The* USHER *takes the mirror.*) Who shut that animal in that cage? Let it out. Have you seen its face behind the bars? There's a poor animal with blood on its head and tears running down its face. Who did that to it? Is it a bird or a horse? It's lying in the dust and its wings are broken. Who broke its wings? Who cut off its hands so that it can't shake the bars? It's pressing its snout on the glass. Who shut that animal in a glass cage? O god, there's no pity in this world. You let it lick the blood from its hair in the corner of a cage with nowhere to hide from its tormentors. No shadow, no hole! Let that animal out of its cage! (*He takes the mirror and shows it round.*) Look! Look! Have pity. Look at its claws trying to open the cage. It's dragging its broken body over the floor. You are cruel! Cruel! Look at it lying in its corner! It's shocked and cut and shaking and licking the blood on its sides. (USHER *again takes the mirror from* LEAR.) No, no! Where are they taking it now! Not out of my sight! What will they do to it? O god, give it to me! Let me hold it and stroke it and wipe its blood! (BODICE *takes the mirror from the* USHER.) No!

BODICE. I'll polish it every day and see it's not cracked.

LEAR. Then kill it. Kill it. Kill it. Don't let her torment it. I can't live with that suffering in the world.

JUDGE. See the king's madness.

LEAR. My daughters have been murdered and these monsters have taken their place! I hear all their victims cry, where is justice?

BODICE. Yes! I've locked this animal in its cage and I will not let it out!

FONTANELLE (*laughing and jumping up and down in her seat*).
Look at his tears!

LEAR. Cruelty! Cruelty! See where they hauled it up by its hair!

BODICE (*to* CLERK). Get it all down!

CLERK. Ma'am.

JUDGE. The court is adjourned.

     LEAR *is taken quickly away, and the court goes.*

LEAR (*going*). Its blood's on the steps where the prisoners come!

    The JUDGE *goes to* BODICE *and* FONTANELLE.

JUDGE. That went better than I expected, ma'am.

BODICE. It went as I planned. There's to be a death sentence but
it's not yet decided. Good day.

    The JUDGE *bows and goes.* BODICE *and* FONTANELLE *are
alone.*

FONTANELLE. It *was* – till your husband interfered.

BODICE. And yours! Keep him on a tighter leash! Well, they must
be brought to sense. Men are always obstinate, it's their form of
maturity. I've bad news. My spies have found agitators and
malcontents in every village. There's going to be serious
fighting – civil war.

FONTANELLE. Good! If it's there let's root it out. Meet it head
on. Did you know this riffraff is commanded by a woman?
Called Cordelia.

BODICE (*aside*). Yes, my sister has her own spies. Power goes to
her head. The head must be squeezed. As it happens, her spies
are in my pay so she can never know more than I know. But
from now on I shall trust her even less. If things go well her
days are numbered. (*To* FONTANELLE.) Well, we'd better go
and see to our husbands. This campaign needs proper preparation.

FONTANELLE. Then we can't leave it to them!

BODICE. And the army must be purged. Victory is bad for soldiers, it lowers their morale.

They go out together.

SCENE TWO

LEAR's *cell.*
Bare, empty. A stone shelf for sitting on. SOLDIERS G *and* H *bring* LEAR *in.* SOLDIER H *drops a roll of sacking on the floor.* SOLDIER G *stands by the door. They ignore* LEAR.

SOLDIER G. Not a bad way t' earn yer livin' if it weren't for the smell.
SOLDIER H. It won't last.
SOLDIER G. Nah, they'll send us up the front with the rest.
SOLDIER H. Cross laddie 'ere off.
    SOLDIER G *marks a list and the* TWO SOLDIERS *go out.*
LEAR. I must forget! I must forget!

> *The* GHOST OF THE GRAVE DIGGER's BOY *appears. His skin and clothes are faded. There's old, dry blood on them.*

GHOST. I heard you shout.
LEAR. Are you dead?
GHOST. Yes.
LEAR. There's an animal in a cage. I must let it out or the earth will be destroyed. There'll be great fires and the water will dry up. All the people will be burned and the wind will blow their ashes into huge columns of dust and they'll go round and round the earth for ever! We must let it out! (*Calls, bangs on the wall.*) Here! Pull your chain! Here! Break it! (*There is banging from the other side of the wall.*) What? It's here! A horse!
GHOST. No. It's other prisoners.
LEAR. Help me!

GHOST. What animal is it? I've never seen it!

LEAR. Where are my daughters! They'd help me!

GHOST. I can fetch them.

LEAR. My daughters? You can fetch them here?

GHOST. Yes.

LEAR. Fetch them! Quickly! (*The* GHOST *whistles softly.*) Where are they?

GHOST. You'll see them. Wait. (*Whistles softly again.*)

> FONTANELLE's GHOST *appears.*

LEAR. Fontanelle!

> GHOST *whistles.* BODICE's GHOST *appears.*

Bodice!

GHOST. Let them speak first.

> *The* DAUGHTERS' GHOSTS *move slowly at first, as if they'd been asleep.*

FONTANELLE. Do my hair . . . Father comes home today.

BODICE. I must put on my dress.

FONTANELLE. O you dress so quickly! Do my hair. (BODICE *attends to her hair.*)

LEAR. My daughters!

BODICE. They're burying soldiers in the churchyard. Father's brought the coffins on carts. The palls are covered with snow. Look, one of the horses is licking its hoof.

FONTANELLE. This morning I lay in bed and watched the wind pulling the curtains. Pull, pull, pull . . . Now I can hear that terrible bell.

LEAR. Fontanelle, you're such a little girl. (*He sits on the stone shelf.*) Sit here.

FONTANELLE. No.

LEAR. On my knees. (*He sits her on his knees.*) Such a little girl.

BODICE (*listening*). Father! I must get dressed! I must get dressed. (*She struggles frantically into her dress.*)

LEAR. That's better.

FONTANELLE. Listen to the bell and the wind.

LEAR (*wets his finger and holds it in the air*). Which way is it blowing? (BODICE *gets into the dress and comes down to him. He points at her.*) Take it off!

BODICE. No.

LEAR. Take it off. Your mother's dress!

BODICE. She's dead! She gave it to me!

LEAR (*pointing*). Take it off!

BODICE. No!

LEAR. Yes, or you will always wear it! (*He pulls her to him.*) Bodice! My poor child, you might as well have worn her shroud.

> BODICE *cries against him.* BEN, *a young orderly, comes in with a small jug and plate. He sets them on the floor.*

BEN. Don't 'ang it out, grandad. They'll be round for the empties in a minute. Don't blame me if it ain't 'ow yer like it. I ain't the chef, I'm only the 'ead waiter.

> BEN *goes out. The* DAUGHTERS' GHOSTS *sit on the floor beside* LEAR *and rest their heads on his knees. He strokes their hair.*

BODICE. Where are we?

LEAR. In a prison.

BODICE. Why?

LEAR. I don't know.

BODICE. Who put us here?

LEAR. I don't know.

FONTANELLE. I'm afraid.

LEAR. Try not to be.

BODICE. Will we get out?

LEAR. Yes.

BODICE. Are you sure?

LEAR. O yes.

BODICE. If I could hope! But this prison, the pain –

LEAR. I know it will end. Everything passes, even the waste. The

fools will be silent. We won't chain ourselves to the dead, or
send our children to school in the graveyard. The torturers and
ministers and priests will lose their office. And we'll pass each
other in the street without shuddering at what we've done to
each other.

BODICE. It's peaceful now.

FONTANELLE. And still.

LEAR. The animal will slip out of its cage, and lie in the fields, and
run by the river, and groom itself in the sun, and sleep in its
hole from night to morning.

> THREE SOLDIERS (G, H *and* I) *come in. They are methodical
> and quiet.*

SOLDIER H. Watch careful an' take it all in.

SOLDIER I. Corp.

SOLDIER H. Under the sack an' in the corners. (SOLDIER G *shows
him how to search.*) Can yer remember it? Five times a day. Yer
skip the personal.

SOLDIER I. Corp.

SOLDIER H. Less see yer try.

SOLDIER I (*searching in the corners*). When yer off?

SOLDIER G. Tmorra. Least it's out a this 'ole.

SOLDIER I. I'll stay out a the fightin' any day!

SOLDIER H. Yer don't know nothin' about it. When there's a war
on yer all end up fightin'.

SOLDIER I (*finishes his search*) Corp.

SOLDIER H. So yer're ready t' mark yer list.

SOLDIER I. Corp. (*Goes to mark his list.*)

SOLDIER H. An' did yer look under the beddin'?

SOLDIER I. Corp.

SOLDIER H. Then look under the beddin'.

SOLDIER I (*looks under the bedding*). Corp.

SOLDIER H. An' now yer can mark yer list.

SOLDIER I. Corp. (*Marks his list.*)

SOLDIER H. Nignogs!... (*When* SOLDIER I *has finished.*) An' on t' the next one.

The THREE SOLDIERS *go out.*

BODICE. Listen. (*She stands.*)

LEAR. Where are you going?

BODICE. Mother's dead. I must serve tea. They're ringing the bell.

LEAR. Stay here.

FONTANELLE. They're waiting. There's a long line behind the coffins. They're standing so still!

LEAR. Stay here and they can't begin. We can stay here together!

GHOST. They must go! You can't stop them!

LEAR. But my mind! My mind!

The DAUGHTERS *go.*

Listen! The animal's scratching! There's blood in its mouth. The muzzle's bleeding. It's trying to dig. It's found someone! (*He falls unconscious on his sack.*)

An OLD ORDERLY *comes in.*

OLD ORDERLY. Sing away, I won't 'urt you. I come for the plate. (*He sees it's untouched.*) O. Shall I come back? Writin' petitions an' appeals an' retainin' yer self respect an' keepin' yer mind occupied – thass all right, but yer must eat. Well, yer know yer own stomach. (*Reassuringly.*) I ain' on the staff. (*Slight pause.*) They're sendin' the young filth up the front. Let 'em rot. Waste a good bullets. I come in 'ere thousands a years back, 'undreds a thousands. I don't know what I come in for. I forgot. I 'eard so many tell what they come in for it's all mixed up in me 'ead. I've 'eard every crime in the book confessed t' me. Must be a record. Don't know which was mine now. Murder? Robbin'? Violence? I'd like t' know. Juss t' put me mind t' rest. Satisfy me conscience. But no one knows now. It's all gone. Long ago. The records is lost. 'Undreds a years back. (*Points to*

plate.) Shall I wait? (*No answer*.) The customer knows what 'e
wants.

The OLD ORDERLY *takes the plate and mug and goes out.*

LEAR. I shouldn't have looked. I killed so many people and never
looked at one of their faces. But I looked at that animal. Wrong.
Wrong. Wrong. It's made me a stupid old man. What colour's
my hair?

GHOST. White.

LEAR. I'm frightened to look. There's blood on it where I pulled
it with these hands.

GHOST. Let me stay with you, Lear. When I died I went somewhere. I don't know where it was. I waited and nothing happened. And then I started to rot, like a body in the ground.
Look at my hands, they're like an old man's. They're withered.
I'm young but my stomach's shrivelled up and the hair's
turned white. Look, my arms! Feel how thin I am. (LEAR
doesn't move.) Are you afraid to touch me?

LEAR. No.

GHOST. Feel.

LEAR (*hesitates. Feels*). Yes, thin.

GHOST. I'm afraid. Let me stay with you, keep me here, please.

LEAR. Yes, yes, poor boy. Lie down by me. Here. I'll hold you.
We'll help each other. Cry while I sleep, and I'll cry and watch
you while you sleep. We'll take turns. The sound of the human
voice will comfort us.

SCENE THREE

Rebel field post.

CORDELIA *and some* REBEL SOLDIERS. PETE *nurses a* WOUNDED
REBEL SOLDIER *called* TERRY. LEWIS *stands upstage as look-out.*
SOLDIER I *sits with his hands tied behind his back and no cap.*
Beside him is a CROUCHING REBEL SOLDIER *with a rifle. Some of*

the other REBEL SOLDIERS *carry rifles. They wear simple, utilitarian clothes, not uniforms. There is a tense silence.*

LEWIS (*looks off*). They're coming.
CORDELIA (*relaxes a little and goes to the* WOUNDED REBEL SOLDIER). Is he all right?
PETE. There's no drugs, no equipment, nothing.

The CARPENTER *comes on with two more* REBEL SOLDIERS. *They carry rifles and bundles.*

CARPENTER. What was the firing?
CORDELIA. Some scouts found us. It's all right, we got them. What did you bring?
CARPENTER. Tea, spuds, two blankets. They won't take money. They want to join us.
CORDELIA. How many?
CARPENTER. Up to twenty.
CORDELIA. Will they bring their own supplies?
CARPENTER. Yes.
CORDELIA. We'll pick them up when we move through. We're almost ready.
CARPENTER (*indicates* SOLDIER I). One of the scouts?
CORDELIA. Yes. The rest were shot. I wanted to talk to him first. Terry was hit.
CARPENTER. O . . .

The two REBEL SOLDIERS *who have just arrived drink tea quickly. The other* REBEL SOLDIERS *carry their bundles off-stage. A* REBEL SOLDIER *hands a mug of tea to the* CARPENTER.

CORDELIA (*to* SOLDIER I). How far did you come?
SOLDIER I. 'Ard t' say. We never come straight an' the maps is US. I was born in the city. These fields are China t' me.
CORDELIA. How long did you march?
SOLDIER I. O I can tell yer that. We moved off at first light.

CARPENTER (*sips his tea*). They've reached the river.

SOLDIER I. Yeh, we come over a river. On a rope – that was a giggle. The farmers'd burned the real bridge. My life!

CORDELIA. What are your supplies like?

SOLDIER I. Nothin'. They used t' be regular. Now everythin's burned. We come through this town. Same thing – burned. Nothin' t' loot. A nice place once.

CORDELIA. Why d'you fight us?

SOLDIER I. I'm more afraid a me own lot than I am a yourn. I'd make a run for it but I'd get a bullet in me back. Not that I'm knockin' your lads! After all, I'm one a you if yer like t' look at it. If I lived out in the sticks I'd be fightin' with you lot, wouldn't I?

>   CORDELIA *and the* CARPENTER *walk away.*

CARPENTER. Let him join us.

CORDELIA. He's a child, he crawls where he's put down. He'd talk to anyone who caught him. To fight like us you must hate, we can't trust a man unless he hates. Otherwise he has no use. (*To* CROUCHING REBEL SOLDIER.) We've finished.

>   CROUCHING REBEL SOLDIER *and* LEWIS *start to take* SOLDIER I *out. Another* SOLDIER *takes* LEWIS's *place as look-out.*

SOLDIER I. 'Ello, we goin' then?

>   *The three go out.* CARPENTER *looks at the* WOUNDED REBEL SOLDIER.

CARPENTER. Where?

PETE. Stomach.

WOUNDED SOLDIER. It's all right, don't whisper. I won't be a nuisance. We said we'd die quietly, if we could. Don't scream or ask for anything. It upsets the others and holds them up . . .

CORDELIA. You must rest before we –

WOUNDED SOLDIER. Yes, yes. Don't treat me like a child because I'm dying. Let me drink some water.

PETE. No.

WOUNDED SOLDIER. It doesn't matter about my stomach. It'll help my throat. (CARPENTER *gives him some water.*) Yes. Now go and get ready.

They leave him and get ready to move.

CORDELIA (*to the* LOOK-OUT). Tell them to start moving. Keep off the road.

The LOOK-OUT *goes out.*

WOUNDED SOLDIER. When it's dark I'll pretend my wife's come to meet me and they're coming up the road. I put our girl on my shoulder and she pulls my hair and I say ah . . .

PETE. More tea?

CARPENTER. No.

PETE empties the tea can and packs it.

WOUNDED SOLDIER. She sees a bird and asks me what it is and I say it's a wader but I don't know . . . Who'll tell my wife I'm dead?

Off, a single shot. No one reacts.

It's dark, there are the stars . . . look . . .

LEWIS *and the* CROUCHING SOLDIER *come back. They pick up their things.*

CORDELIA. When we have power these things won't be necessary.

Everyone goes off except the WOUNDED SOLDIER.

WOUNDED SOLDIER. The stars . . . Look . . . One . . . Two . . . Three . . .

Silence.

SCENE FOUR

HQ.

BODICE *sleeps slumped forward over a desk. On the desk a map,*
documents, pen, ink, teacher's bell. By the desk, BODICE's *knitting*
bag full of documents. Off, a knock. BODICE *hears and moves but*
doesn't sit up. Off, a second knock. BODICE *sits up and rings the bell*
once. An AIDE *comes in.*

AIDE. Your sister's here now, ma'am.
BODICE. What time is it?
AIDE. Two.
BODICE. Let her in.

AIDE *lets* FONTANELLE *in and goes out.*

FONTANELLE. Your aide says our husbands have run away!
BODICE. They met the Chiefs of Staff this afternoon. The army
thinks we'll lose the war.
FONTANELLE. Impossible. We're fighting peasants.
BODICE. The army thinks –
FONTANELLE. They can't think! Our husbands ran our campaign,
that's why we lost. But if they're gone now, we'll win!
BODICE. You silly woman, haven't you learned anything yet? I
had to send troops to bring them back. They're downstairs now.
FONTANELLE. Why?
BODICE. Why? We need their armies!
FONTANELLE. O – they'll fight for us!
BODICE. They wouldn't break a grasshopper's leg for us. Why
d'you think I put up with my husband for so long?
FONTANELLE. Put up with him?
BODICE. O don't waste your hypocrisy on me. You tried to kill
yours once. My spies told me and they don't lie. They're the
only moral institution in this country.
FONTANELLE (*shrugs*). Well, I don't bother any more. He's
stopped slobbering over me and I sleep with whom I like.

BODICE. It must be getting difficult to find someone.

FONTANELLE (*after a pause, in a small voice*). Well I don't wake them up in the middle of the night to ask them to hold my wool. Is that why you sleep alone?

BODICE. At least they'd get to sleep first. Sign these before you go.

FONT.:NELLE. What are they?

BODICE. Various warrants. We'll have to run the country between us – but you're no good at office work, it's a waste of time you trying.

FONTANELLE. I'll only sign what doesn't conflict with my conscience. (*Picks up a document.*) What's this?

BODICE. Father's death warrant.

FONTANELLE. Where's the pen?

BODICE (*as FONTANELLE signs*). There are a number of old matters it's politically dangerous to leave open. They should have been closed long ago, but it's been left to us, of course!

FONTANELLE. Where is he?

BODICE. They're bringing a batch of prisoners to HQ. They had to evacuate the prisons. The warrants will be carried out when they arrive. Sign the others.

A signal is tapped on the door. BODICE *rings the bell once.* TWO PLAINCLOTHES SPIES *bring the* DUKES OF CORNWALL *and* NORTH *in. They have been questioned but not marked. Their jackets, belts and laces have been removed. They look flushed.* BODICE *stands.*

No – be silent! Not one word! There's nothing to explain. My spies have learned more about you than you know yourselves, and none of it came as a surprise to me.

FONTANELLE. Burn them!

BODICE. Be quiet! You will be kept in cells until we need you to be seen in public, or for any other reason. (NORTH *opens his mouth to speak.*) Be quiet! While you are out of your cells you will at all times be accompanied by my plainclothes spies. If you misbehave in any way you will be instantly shot. (NORTH

opens his mouth to speak.) Will you be quiet! – We would explain
it away as an assassination by the enemy.
FONTANELLE. Burn them! I'm superstitious, they'll bring us bad
luck.
BODICE. Take them downstairs.

> The TWO PLAINCLOTHES SPIES *take the* DUKES OF NORTH
> *and* CORNWALL *out.*

FONTANELLE. And what will you do about the war?
BODICE (*rings the bell once*). You'd better go back to bed. You
mustn't keep your chauffeur waiting.

> FONTANELLE *goes towards the door and meets the* AIDE
> *coming in.*

FONTANELLE. Major Pellet, don't let my sister overwork you.
AIDE. We're very busy, ma'am.
FONTANELLE. If she bullies you let me know.
AIDE. Ma'am.

> FONTANELLE *goes out.* BODICE *hands him the warrants.*

BODICE. Hand these to the adjutant. Morning will do.
AIDE. Yes, ma'am.

> *The* AIDE *goes out.* BODICE *looks at the map.*

BODICE. War. Power. (*Off*, FONTANELLE *laughs briefly, and then
the* AIDE *laughs briefly.*) I'm forced to sit at this desk, work with
my sister, walk beside my husband. They say decide this and
that, but I don't decide anything. My decisions are forced on
me. I change people's lives and things get done – it's like a
mountain moving forward, but not because I tell it to. I started
to pull the wall down, and I had to stop that – the men are
needed here. (*She taps the map with the finger tips of one hand.*)
And now I must move them here and here – (*She moves her
index finger on the map.*) – because the map's my straitjacket and
that's all I can do. I'm trapped. (*Off, a clock strikes rapidly.
Silence. She thinks about her life, but not reflectively. She is*

trying to understand what has happened to her.) I hated being a girl, but at least I was happy sometimes. And it was better when I grew up, I could be myself – they didn't humiliate me then. I was almost free! I made so many plans, one day I'd be my own master! Now I have all the power . . . and I'm a slave. Worse! (*Rings the bell once.*) Pellet! – I shall work. I shall pounce on every mistake my enemy makes! (*Rings the bell once.*) War is so full of chances! I only need a little luck. (*Rings the bell twice.*) Pellet! Pellet! (*Picks up the map and starts to go.*) Are you asleep?

    She goes out.

SCENE FIVE

Road.
Prison convoy on a country road. LEAR *and* FOUR PRISONERS *chained together by the neck and blindfolded.* LEAR *is also gagged. They are led and guarded by* THREE SOLDIERS (J, K *and* L). *Everyone is tired and dirty. They talk nervously and quietly, all except* LEAR. *Continuous heavy gun fire in the distance.*

SOLDIER J (*looking at a map*). Useless bloody map!
SOLDIER K (*looks round*). We're lost!
SOLDIER J. Shut up! (*To* PRISONERS.) Hup hup!
FIRST PRISONER (*quietly*). Can't go anymore.
SECOND PRISONER. Lean on me.
SOLDIER K. Hup.
THIRD PRISONER (*to* SECOND PRISONER). Let 'im go. 'E knows when e's 'ad enough.
SOLDIER L. Hup.
SECOND PRISONER. No. They'll shoot him.
SOLDIER K. We're 'eadin' back the way we come.
SOLDIER J. 'Alt! (*The* PRISONERS *stop immediately.*) Down. (*They sit. To* SOLDIER K.) Go 'an 'ave a little reccy. You're good at directions.

> SOLDIER K *goes out. The* PRISONERS *pass round a water can.*
> *They don't remove their blindfolds.*

FOURTH PRISONER. I'm next.

SOLDIER J (*crouches and studies map*). They must a issued this for
the Crimea.

SECOND PRISONER (*gives water to* FIRST PRISONER). I'll hold
it.

SOLDIER L. I tol' yer t' wrap it.

SOLDIER J. Wha' direction's the firin' comin' from?

SOLDIER L. Moves about.

SECOND PRISONER. Enough.

FIRST PRISONER. Thank you.

SECOND PRISONER. I'll try to look where we are. Keep in front
of me.

FOURTH PRISONER. Here. (*The water can is passed to him. It's
almost empty.*) Bastards! It's empty! (*Drinks.*)

THIRD PRISONER. Leave some. (*Takes the water can.*)

SOLDIER L (*sees* SECOND PRISONER *trying to look*). Oi wass your
game!

SOLDIER J. Wass up?

SECOND PRISONER. Nothing. Nothing.

SOLDIER L. I saw yer look.

SECOND PRISONER. No.

SOLDIER J. 'E look?

SOLDIER L. Yeh! Any more out a you and yer'll look through a 'ole
in yer 'ead. I got the enemy breathin' up me arse. I ain' messin'
about with you, sonny.

> *The* TWO SOLDIERS *go back to the map.*

SOLDIER J (*looking off*). Wass keepin' 'im?

SOLDIER L. Don't tell me 'e's gone an' got lost now. Why don't we
run for it?

SOLDIER J (*indicates* PRISONERS). What about these darlin's?

SOLDIER L. Leave 'em, kill 'em.

SOLDIER J. Give it another minute. Best t' stick t' orders as long as yer can.

SOLDIER L (*grumbling nastily*). I ain' cartin' this garbage round much longer, we ain' safe ourselves. (*Suddenly calls after* SOLDIER K, *low and intense*.) Billy? (*Silence*.) 'E don't 'ear. Reckon 'e's scarpered?

SOLDIER J. Billy? Nah.

THIRD PRISONER (*removes gag from* LEAR'*s mouth and holds the water can against it*). 'Ere, drink this an' be quiet.

LEAR (*after drinking a mouthful*). More.

FOURTH PRISONER. It's gone.

LEAR. I can't see.

THIRD PRISONER. Our eyes are covered.

LEAR. Where are we?

SOLDIER L. Joker. 'Oo unplugged 'is gob?

LEAR (*loudly and serenely*). Why do they pull me about like this? Why do they waste their time on me. If they let me I'd go away quietly. How could I harm them? They're young, why do they waste their life leading an old man on a rope?

The distant guns sound louder.

SOLDIER L. 'Ark at it! (*Calls as before*.) Billy?

SOLDIER J. Leave it.

SOLDIER L. I'll go an' look for 'im.

SOLDIER J. O no you don't.

LEAR. I've lost my boy.

SOLDIER L (*to* PRISONERS). I ain' warnin' yer. Keep 'im quiet.

LEAR. There are so many voices! I must find him. I had a terrible pain in my head and he stopped it and now I must help him. He's lost. He needs me. What will they do to him if I'm not there to call them off? Boy! Boy! Hey!

SOLDIER L. All right, bloody 'ush!

LEAR (*stands*). Here! Here!

FOURTH PRISONER. Stop him! My neck!

SOLDIER J. E's bloody mad!

FOURTH PRISONER. Kick him!

SOLDIER L (*runs to* LEAR *and gags him*). I said stow it, grandad.
  Now bloody talk t' yerself. (*He goes back to* SOLDIER J, *who is
  still by the map.*) Get yer rifle. They've 'ad long enough.

SOLDIER J. Give 'em a little bit longer. (*He kneels in front of the
  map.*) We must be on 'ere somewhere.

> *Pause.* LEAR *makes sounds through his gag. Slowly* SOLDIERS
> J *and* L *raise their hands over their heads – they look like
> Moslems about to pray.* SOLDIER K *comes on with his hands
> above his head. They stay like this in silence for a few moments.
> The* CARPENTER, LEWIS, PETE *and other* REBEL SOLDIERS
> *come on. They are quick, quiet and tense.*

CARPENTER. This them?

SOLDIER K. Yeh.

> LEWIS *goes upstage as Look Out. A* REBEL SOLDIER *picks up*
> SOLDIERS J *and* L's *rifles.*

CARPENTER. Anyone in charge?

SOLDIER J. 'Ere.

CARPENTER. Where were you wanting to get to?

SOLDIER J. HQ. Evacuating that lot.

CARPENTER. You haven't got an HQ left.

FOURTH PRISONER (*takes off his blindfold*). We're free . . . (*The
  PRISONERS hesitate awkwardly.*) Can we take the chains
  off?

CARPENTER. No. Not till the political officers have been through
  you. (*Points to* SOLDIERS J, K *and* L.) Tie them up.

> *The* THREE SOLDIER's *hands are tied behind their backs. The*
> CARPENTER *goes to the side of the stage, whistles, and gestures
> to someone to come on.*

FOURTH PRISONER. You can undo me. I'm a political prisoner.
  On your side. I shall have influence when things are changed.
  I'll put in a word for you soldiers. You've saved my life.

FONTANELLE *and a* REBEL SOLDIER *come on from the direction of the* CARPENTER's *whistle. Her hands are tied behind her back. She is dirty and dishevelled and her clothes are torn.*

CARPENTER. Tie her on the end.

PETE (*tying* FONTANELLE *on to the chain of* PRISONERS). Can they take their blindfolds off?

CARPENTER. If you like.

The PRISONERS *remove their blindfolds.* THIRD PRISONER *takes* LEAR's *off.*

LEAR. Undo this chain. My hands are white. There's no blood in them. My neck's like old leather. You'd have a job to hang me now. I don't want to live except for the boy. Who'd look after him?

FONTANELLE. Don't tie me up with him! (*Cries with anger.*) O God, how foul . . .

LEAR. Who's crying? (*Still serenely. He doesn't recognize her.*) Stop that, child. Ask them quietly. You're a woman, you should know how to do that. Some of them are kind, some of them listen.

FONTANELLE. You stupid, stupid, wicked fool!

LEAR. You mustn't shout. No one will listen to that. They all shout here.

CARPENTER. Who is he? I've seen him before.

SOLDIER J. Don't know any of 'em from Adam. That one thinks 'e's king.

CARPENTER. It'd be safer to be Jesus Christ.

Off, a whistle.

LEWIS. We're off. (*He whistles back.*)

PETE. On your feet. (*The* PRISONERS *stand.*)

FONTANELLE. Don't take me like this. The people will throw stones at me and shout. They hate me. I'm afraid. I'll faint and scream. I've never been humiliated, I don't know how to behave. Help me. Please.

LEAR. Don't ask them for favours. Walk with us. Be gentle and don't pull.

CARPENTER. Watch that old one. He's a trouble maker.

LEAR. We'll go decently and quietly and look for my boy. He was very good to me. He saved my mind when I went mad. And to tell you the truth I did him a great wrong once, a very great wrong. He's never blamed me. I must be kind to him now. Come on, we'll find him together.

They go out in the direction from which the PRISONERS *came on.*

SCENE SIX

LEAR's *second cell.*
It is darker than before. LEAR, FONTANELLE *and the* PRISONERS *from the chain gang (except* FOURTH PRISONER*) are sitting on the ground. A bare electric bulb hangs from the ceiling. It is unlit. Off, a sudden burst of rifle shots.*

FIRST PRISONER (*jumps up*). They're starting again!

SECOND PRISONER. No. They said last week it was only once. They got rid of the undesirables then. (*Trying to sound calm.*) We mustn't panic.

The OLD ORDERLY *comes on with a bucket and puts it down upstage.*

THIRD PRISONER. Yeh, they're still feedin' us. They wouldn't waste grub . . .

SECOND PRISONER (*to* OLD ORDERLY). What are they doing?

OLD ORDERLY. Never noticed.

FIRST PRISONER. We heard shooting.

OLD ORDERLY. Could 'ave. My 'earin' went 'undred a years back.

THIRD PRISONER. Why are they keepin' us 'ere? We should a bin out by now.

OLD ORDERLY. No orders, no papers, no forms, nothing comes through – no one knows what to do.

The OLD ORDERLY *goes out. Everyone eats except* LEAR *and* FIRST PRISONER. *They watch each other hungrily while they eat.* FONTANELLE *only eats a little.* LEAR *sits on the ground. He is still calm and remote.*

SECOND PRISONER (*jostling at the bucket*). Steady!

The GRAVEDIGGER'S BOY'S GHOST *comes on. He is white and thin.*

LEAR. Where have you been? Are you in pain?

GHOST. What? I don't know. I'm so cold. See how thin I am. Look at my legs. I think my chest's empty inside. Where have you been?

LEAR. Some men took us out of the town and along a road and some more men stopped us and brought us back again. I was lonely without you and worried, but I knew I'd find you. (LEAR *and the* GHOST *sit and lean against each other.*)

GHOST. Tell me what you saw. This city's like a grave. I tried to follow you but when we got out in the open the wind was too strong, it pushed me back.

LEAR. There was so much sky. I could hardly see. I've always looked down at the hills and banks where the enemy was hiding. But there's only a little strip of earth and all the sky. You're like my son now. I wish I'd been your father. I'd have looked after you so well.

The COMMANDANT, OLD ORDERLY *and* THREE SOLDIERS (M, N *and* O) *come in. The* SOLDIERS *carry rifles.*

COMMANDANT. What's that food bucket doing here?

OLD ORDERLY. They're always fed at this time. It's on standin'
  orders.
COMMANDANT. You old fool. (*Reads from a list.*) Evans.
THIRD PRISONER. Yeh.
COMMANDANT. M413. Leave that. L37 Hewit.
SECOND PRISONER. Yes.
COMMANDANT. H257 Wellstone.
FIRST PRISONER. Yes.
COMMANDANT. Outside.
SOLDIER M. Get fell in sharp.
SECOND PRISONER. We're on the wrong list.
SOLDIER N. Tell me that outside.
THIRD PRISONER. We're politicals.
SECOND PRISONER. I was on your side. That's why I'm here.
COMMANDANT. It's all been cleared up. You're transferees. Out-
  side, there's good lads.
SECOND PRISONER. No.

> SOLDIERS M *and* N *run* SECOND PRISONER *out. He shouts
> 'No!' once more before he goes.* COMMANDANT *and* SOLDIER
> O *take* FIRST *and* THIRD PRISONERS *outside. The* OLD
> ORDERLY *picks up some scraps of food from the floor and drops
> them in the bucket.* LEAR *goes to the bucket to feed.*

OLD ORDERLY. Throw their muck anywhere.
FONTANELLE. For as long as I can remember there was misery
  and waste and suffering wherever you were. You live in your
  own mad world, you can't hear me. You've wasted my life and
  I can't even tell you. O god, where can I find justice?
LEAR. They didn't leave much.

> *Off, a burst of rifle shots.*

OLD ORDERLY. Do this, run there, fetch that, carry this. Finished?
  (*He picks up the bucket.*) No one can put a foot right today. Job
  like this upsets the whole place. (*Starts to go.*) Work. Work.
  Work.

The OLD ORDERLY *goes out.* FONTANELLE *goes to* LEAR.

FONTANELLE. Talk to them! Say you know something the government ought to know. Promise them something. Anything. Make them – negotiate! – put us on trial! O father, you must think!

LEAR. He's taken the bucket. I always scrape it.

FONTANELLE. Bodice is still fighting. She'll beat them, she always does. Help me, father. If Bodice saves us I'll look after you. I understand you now. Take everything back. God knows I don't want it. Look, let me help you. Father, think. Try. Talk to them, argue with them – you're so good at that. Sit down. (*She brushes hair from his face.*) We mustn't shout at each other. I do love you. I'm such a stupid woman. Yes (*She laughs.*) – stupid, stupid! But you understand me. What will you say to them?

LEAR. All the sky.

FONTANELLE. Remember! Remember!

LEAR. And a little piece of earth.

The CARPENTER, COMMANDANT, OLD ORDERLY, FOURTH PRISONER *and* SOLDIERS M, N *and* O *come in.* FOURTH PRISONER *wears a crumpled, dark-blue striped suit.*

COMMANDANT (*to* SOLDIERS, *indicating the cell*). Keep this one separate for the family.

FONTANELLE. Are you putting us on trial?

CARPENTER. Your father's case is still open. But yours has been closed.

FONTANELLE (*calmer*). If I appealed it would go to you?

CARPENTER. Yes.

FONTANELLE. My sister will punish you if you do anything to us!

CARPENTER. We've got her. We're bringing her here.

Off, a burst of rifle shots.

FONTANELLE (*agitated again*). Let me swallow poison. You don't

care how I die as long as you get rid of me. Why must you hurt
me?

CARPENTER (*shakes his head*). No. I can't stay long and I must see
it finished. I have to identify the body.

> SOLDIER N *shoots* FONTANELLE *from behind. She falls dead
> immediately.*

COMMANDANT. Will you wait in my office? It's warmer.

CARPENTER. Thank you.

> *The* COMMANDANT *and* CARPENTER *go out wearily.*
> SOLDIERS M *and* N *follow them.* LEAR, GHOST, FOURTH
> PRISONER *and* SOLDIER O *are left.* SOLDIER O *helps* FOURTH
> PRISONER *to erect a trestle table.*

FOURTH PRISONER. Bring this here.

> SOLDIER O *helps* FOURTH PRISONER *to put* FONTA-
> NELLE'*s body on the table. They move quietly and efficiently.*
> FOURTH PRISONER *switches on the bare electric light over the
> table. He has turned his white shirt-cuffs back over his jacket
> sleeves. The* GHOST *cringes away.* LEAR *stares at* FOURTH
> PRISONER. *Slowly he stands. He begins to see where he is.*

GHOST. It's beginning.

LEAR. What?

GHOST. Quickly, Lear! I'll take you away! We'll go to the place
where I was lost!

LEAR. No. I ran away so often, but my life was ruined just the
same. Now I'll stay. (*He stares at* FOURTH PRISONER.)

FOURTH PRISONER (*efficiently*). I'm the prison medical doctor.
We met in less happy times. I said I was in good standing with
the government. My papers confirmed that. I'm just waiting for
more papers and then I'll be given a post of more obvious trust
and importance. We're ready to begin.

LEAR. What are you doing?

FOURTH PRISONER. A little autopsy. Not a big one. We know
what she died of. But I handle this routine work methodically.

Otherwise they think you can't be trusted with bigger things. My new papers will open up many new opportunities for me.

LEAR. Who was she?

FOURTH PRISONER. Your daughter.

LEAR. Did I have a daughter?

FOURTH PRISONER. Yes, it's on her chart. That's her stomach and the liver underneath. I'm just making a few incisions to satisfy the authorities.

LEAR. Is that my daughter . . .? (*Points.*) That's . . .?

FOURTH PRISONER. The stomach.

LEAR (*points*). That?

FOURTH PRISONER. The lungs. You can see how she died. The bullet track goes through the lady's lungs.

LEAR. But where is the . . . She was cruel and angry and hard . . .

FOURTH PRISONER (*points*). The womb.

LEAR. So much blood and bits and pieces packed in with all that care. Where is the . . . where . . .?

FOURTH PRISONER. What is the question?

LEAR. Where is the beast? The blood is as still as a lake. Where . . .? Where . . .?

FOURTH PRISONER (*to* SOLDIER O). What's the man asking? (*No response.*)

LEAR. She sleeps inside like a lion and a lamb and a child. The things are so beautiful. I am astonished. I have never seen anything so beautiful. If I had known she was so beautiful . . . Her body was made by the hand of a child, so sure and nothing unclean . . . If I had known this beauty and patience and care, how I would have loved her.

The GHOST *starts to cry but remains perfectly still.*

Did I make this – and destroy it?

BODICE *is brought in by* SOLDIERS M *and* N. *She is dirty and dishevelled, but she has tried to clean herself and tidy her hair. She tries to sound eager and in control.*

BODICE. In here? Yes. Thank you. Did my letter go to the government?

SOLDIER M. Wait 'ere.

BODICE. Yes. Thank you. I must see someone in authority. I want to explain my letter, you see. (*Sees* LEAR.) O, yes, they've put us together. That must be a friendly sign. Now I know they mean to act properly!

FOURTH PRISONER. Pass me my forms. (SOLDIER O *hands him some forms.*)

BODICE (*brightly trying to show interest*). What are you doing?

LEAR. That's your sister.

BODICE. No!

LEAR. I destroyed her.

BODICE. Destroyed? No, no! We admit nothing. We acted for the best. Did what we had to do.

LEAR. I destroyed her! I knew nothing, saw nothing, learned nothing! Fool! Fool! Worse than I knew! (*He puts his hands into* FONTANELLE *and brings them out covered with dark blood and smeared with viscera. The* SOLDIERS *react awkwardly and ineffectually.*) Look at my dead daughter!

BODICE. No! No!

LEAR. Look! I killed her! Her blood is on my hands! Destroyer! Murderer! And now I must begin again. I must walk through my life, step after step, I must walk in weariness and bitterness, I must become a child, hungry and stripped and shivering in blood, I must open my eyes and see!

The COMMANDANT *runs in shouting and pointing at the* SOLDIERS.

COMMANDANT. You! – You! – What is this? Get it under control!

FOURTH PRISONER. I tried to stop them – saboteurs! – don't let this stop my petition –

The CARPENTER *comes in.*

BODICE. Thank god! At last! I wrote to your wife. She's sent you to me. She accepts my offer to collaborate. I was against the fighting. I can show you minutes. My father's mad, you can see that – and my sister drove him on!

CARPENTER. The government found no extenuating circumstances in your case.

BODICE. O – but you haven't been told everything. You must acquaint yourself with the facts. No, I don't expect you to let me go. I'm culpable by association. I've been foolish. I accept that. Now there must be a term of imprisonment. I fully accept it.

CARPENTER. You were sentenced to death.

BODICE. No! You have no right! I will not be dealt with by your – committee! I have a right to justice in court! O you are cruel when you get a little power – when you have the power I had you beg people to accept your mercy so that god will not judge you! (*Falls down.*) Please. Please. Please.

CARPENTER. Be quick.

> SOLDIER N *moves behind* BODICE *with a pistol. She sees him and fights furiously.* SOLDIER M *and* O *join in. They can't see to aim.* SOLDIER O *fixes a bayonet.* BODICE *bites* SOLDIER M.

SOLDIER M. Bitch!

> SOLDIER M *throws her to the ground again. She writhes away and screams.*

'Old 'er still!

> SOLDIER N *kicks her.* SOLDIERS M *and* N *pinion her with their boots. She writhes and screams.*

'Old 'er! 'Old 'er!

> SOLDIER O *bayonets her three times. Slight pause. She writhes. He bayonets her once again. She gives a spasm and dies.*

CARPENTER. Thank you. I'm sorry. You're good lads.

SOLDIER O. . . . . Blimey.

COMMANDANT (*to* SOLDIERS). Clear up, lads.

> *The* CARPENTER *starts to go. The* COMMANDANT *stops him.*
> *While the* COMMANDANT *and the* CARPENTER *talk,* SOL-
> DIERS *remove* FONTANELLE, BODICE *and the trestle table*

(*He tries to force the* CARPENTER.) We should finish everything. There's still the old man.

CARPENTER. You know I can't. My wife says no. She knew him.

COMMANDANT. I've been having a word with the prison MO.
Very reliable man, sir. (*He beckons* FOURTH PRISONER *over.*)
About the old one.

FOURTH PRISONER. If he has to be kept alive –

CARPENTER. I've already explained that –

FOURTH PRISONER. I follow, sir. Then he could be made
politically ineffective.

CARPENTER. What does that mean?

FOURTH PRISONER. Madmen often harm themselves.

CARPENTER. But not killed. That's too obvious.

FOURTH PRISONER. Only harmed.

CARPENTER. Well, anything happens in a war.

COMMANDANT. Good.

> *The* COMMANDANT *and* CARPENTER *go out.*

FOURTH PRISONER. This is a chance to bring myself to notice.

> FOURTH PRISONER *goes upstage into the dark.*

SOLDIER M. She bit me. What yer do for snake bite?

SOLDIER N (*looks*). I'd burn that.

SOLDIER O. Thass only a dose a rabbies.

> FOURTH PRISONER *comes downstage with a heap of equipment.*
> *The* GHOST *stands and watches silently.* LEAR *is immobile.*
> *He is completely withdrawn.*

FOURTH PRISONER. Right. (*He goes to* LEAR.) Good morning. Time for your drive. Into your coat. (LEAR *is put into a strait-jacket. He doesn't help in any way.*) Cross your arms and hold your regalia. Now the buttons. This nasty wind gets in everywhere. You've been inside too long to trust yourself to fresh air. (LEAR *is seated on a chair.*) Get settled down. (*His legs are strapped to the chair legs.*) And last your crown. (*A square frame is lowered over his head and face.* FOURTH PRISONER *steps back. Then* LEAR *speaks.*)

LEAR. You've turned me into a king again.

FOURTH PRISONER (*produces a tool*). Here's a device I perfected on dogs for removing human eyes.

LEAR. No, no. You mustn't touch my eyes. I must have my eyes!

FOURTH PRISONER. With this device you extract the eye undamaged and then it can be put to good use. It's based on a scouting gadget I had as a boy.

SOLDIER N. Get on. It's late.

FOURTH PRISONER. Understand, this isn't an instrument of torture, but a scientific device. See how it clips the lid back to leave it unmarked.

LEAR. No – no!

FOURTH PRISONER. Nice and steady. (*He removes one of* LEAR's *eyes.*)

LEAR. Aahh!

FOURTH PRISONER. Note how the eye passes into the lower chamber and is received into a soothing solution of formaldehyde crystals. One more, please. (*He removes* LEAR's *other eye.*)

LEAR. Aaahhh!

FOURTH PRISONER (*looking at the eyes in the glass container*). Perfect.

LEAR (*jerking in the chair*). Aaahhh! The sun! It hurts my eyes!

FOURTH PRISONER (*sprays an aerosol into* LEAR's *eye sockets*). That will assist the formation of scab and discourage flies. (*To* SOLDIERS.) Clean this up with a bucket and mop.

FOURTH PRISONER *starts to leave.*

LEAR. Aaahhh! It hurts!
FOURTH PRISONER. Keep still. You make it worse.

    FOURTH PRISONER *goes out.*

SOLDIER M. Less get away an' shut the door.
SOLDIER N. 'E'll 'ave the 'ole bloody place up.
SOLDIER O. O lor.

   The THREE SOLDIERS *go out.* LEAR *and the* GHOST *are left.*

LEAR. Aaahhh! The roaring in my head. I see blood. (*Spits.*)
    Blood in my mouth. (*Jerks.*) My hands – undo my hands and
    let me kill myself.
GHOST. Lear.
LEAR. Who's that! What d'you want? You can't take my eyes, but
    take the rest! Kill me! Kill me!
GHOST. No – people will be kind to you now. Surely you've
    suffered enough.
LEAR. You. (*The* GHOST *starts to unfasten* LEAR.) Tell me the pain
    will stop! This pain must stop! O stop, stop, stop!
GHOST. It will stop. Sometimes it might come back, but you'll
    learn to bear it. I can stay with you now you need me.
LEAR. Wipe my mouth. There's blood. I'm swallowing blood.
GHOST. Stand. Please. (LEAR *stumbles to his feet.*) Walk as if you
    could see. Try. We'll go back to my house. It's quiet there,
    they'll leave you in peace at last.
LEAR (*stumbling forward*). Take me away! This pain must stop!
    Ah! (*Stumbling out.*) Take me somewhere to die!

    LEAR *stumbles out with the* GHOST.

SCENE SEVEN

Near the wall.
Open fields.
A FARMER, *his* WIFE *and* SON *hurry on. They cross upstage. They carry bundles.*

SON. Doo come. Thass late.
FARMER'S WIFE. Don't fret. Goo on, we'll keep up.
> LEAR *stumbles on downstage with the* GHOST. LEAR *now carries a stick.*
LEAR. Where are we, where are we? The wind's stinging my eyes. They're full of dust.
GHOST. We're near the wall. It'll be easier to walk along the top. Stop. There's some people here. Shall we hide in the scrub?
LEAR. No. I must beg.

> LEAR *takes out a bowl and begs.*

Alms! I'm not a criminal, I wasn't blinded by a judge. Alms!

> *The* FARMER, *his* WIFE *and* SON *come down to* LEAR.

FARMER. Good day, father. (*He looks at the bowl. His* SON *makes a gesture of refusal.*) We ont got no bait for yoo. We're poor people off the land. Thass my wife an' my littl' ol' boy by me here.
LEAR. Can I rest in your house? I'm so tired.
FARMER. Yoo'd be welcome an' more, but thass gone. See, sir, when the ol' king went mad they stop buildin' his wall, an' a great crowd a people come up these parts. The ol' king cleared a good strip a land both sides his wall. Rare land that was. So we took a plow an' built ourselves homes.
FARMER'S WIFE. An' now they're buildin' the wall again, count a the govermin's changed.
FARMER. So the soldier boys turned us out on our land. Now everyone's off to the work camp to work on the wall. We'd best move sharp, do there'll be no more room.

FARMER'S WIFE. The women as well.

FARMER. An' the boy's off to be a soldier.

FARMER'S WIFE. We can't bait en an' dress en n' more.

LEAR. But they'll kill him in the army.

FARMER'S WIFE. We must hope they won't.

SON. Thass late. T'ent time t' natter. Doo come.

> *The* SON *goes out.*

FARMER'S WIFE. We're speedin', boy.

> *The* FARMER *and his* WIFE *go out after their* SON.

LEAR. I could learn to endure my blindness with patience, I
could never endure this! (*Calls.*) Children! Ah!

> LEAR *falls down on to his knees.*

FARMER'S WIFE (*off*). The poor gentleman's toppled over.

> *The* FARMER *and his* WIFE *and* SON *hurry on.*

LEAR. I am the King! I kneel by this wall. How many lives have I
ended here? Go away. Go anywhere. Go far away. Run. I will
not move till you go!

FARMER'S WIFE. Do stand, sir.

LEAR. I've heard your voices. I'd never seen a poor man! You take
too much pity out of me, if there's no pity I shall die of this
grief.

SON. That ol' boy's a great rambler.

LEAR. They feed you and clothe you – is that why you can't
see? All life seeks its safety. A wolf, a fox, a horse – they'd run
away, they're sane. Why d'you run to meet your butchers?
Why?

SON. I'll see you in the camp.

> *The* FARMER'S SON *goes out.*

FARMER'S WIFE. Tent decent leavin' en out here on his own, dad.

FARMER. Poor man. If yoo take en someplace they'll beat en an' chain en. Let en be, he's at home in the fields. Let en bear his cross in peace.

The FARMER *and the* FARMER'S WIFE *go out.*

LEAR (*stumbles to his feet*). Men destroy themselves and say it's their duty? It's not possible! How can they be so abused? Cordelia doesn't know what she's doing! I must tell her – write to her!

GHOST. No, no, no! They never listen!

LEAR. I can't be silent! O my eyes! This crying's opened my wounds! There's blood again! Quick, quick, help me! My eyes, my eyes! I must stop her before I die!

LEAR *stumbles out on the* GHOST'S *arm.*

Act Three

SCENE ONE

The GRAVEDIGGER'S BOY'S *house.*
More dilapidated, but obviously lived in. The stage is empty for a moment. THOMAS *and* JOHN *come in.*

THOMAS (*calls*). We're home! (*Stretches and yawns happily.*) I'm all in.

> JOHN *draws water from the well and washes himself.* SUSAN *comes to the door with* LEAR. THOMAS *embraces her.*

SUSAN. Have you been busy?

LEAR. No news from the village?

THOMAS. No.

LEAR. None? (THOMAS *starts to lead* LEAR *to a bench.*) Cordelia should have answered my last letter. It was stronger than the others. I thought she'd have to answer –

THOMAS (*calming him*). I know, I know.

JOHN. I'll eat in the village tonight with my girl's family.

SUSAN (*slightly annoyed*). You should have told me. (*To* THOMAS.) It won't be long.

THOMAS. I'm starving!

> SUSAN *goes into the house with* THOMAS. JOHN *throws his water away. A* SMALL MAN *comes in. He is dirty and frightened and in rags.*

SMALL MAN. I was lookin' – for someone. Could you give us some water?

> JOHN *nods to a pitcher by the well. The* SMALL MAN *drinks noisily.*

JOHN. You're off the road.

SMALL MAN (*sees* LEAR). Ah, sir. It was you I was lookin' for, sir.
They said – (*He stops.*) You knew me when I was a soldier, sir.
Small dark man. Black hair.

LEAR. What's your name?

SMALL MAN. O yes. McFearson.

JOHN. How did you get in that state?

> THOMAS *comes out of the house. He puts his hand on* LEAR's
> *shoulder.*

SMALL MAN. On the road. Thass why I'm 'ungry.

LEAR. Yes, I think I remember you. If you're hungry you'd better
stay to dinner.

SMALL MAN. Thank you, thanks.

LEAR. Give him John's. He's going down to the village. Take him
into the house.

> THOMAS *takes the* SMALL MAN *into the house.* THOMAS *turns
> in the doorway.*

THOMAS (*to* LEAR). He can't stay. Apart from anything else there
isn't enough food.

LEAR. I'll tell him.

> THOMAS *goes on into the house. The* GHOST *has come on. He
> looks thinner and more wasted.*

GHOST. D'you know who he is?

LEAR. A soldier.

> JOHN *turns to watch* LEAR.

GHOST. That's right, a deserter. I suppose the fool didn't keep out
of sight, moved by day, asked everyone where you were. It
won't take them long to follow him. Get rid of the lot of them!
Then we'll be safe.

> *The* SMALL MAN *comes out of the house.*

SMALL MAN. Didn't want to get under the lady's feet. It's good of you to let me – (*He stops.*) I thought, for old time's sake . . . The 'ole regiment said you was one a the best.

JOHN (*putting on his jacket*). I'm off.

> JOHN *goes and the* SMALL MAN *immediately sits down on the bench.*

SMALL MAN. Good old days, really. (*Laughs.*) Only yer never know it at the time. Nice 'ere, nice place. You're very well fixed – considerin'.

LEAR. Yes.

SMALL MAN. Mind you, yer must be hard pressed. Not a lot t' do everythin'. Juss the two men an' the girl, is it? (*No reply.*) An' you must take a fair bit a lookin' after. An' why shouldn't yer be looked after? Yer deserve it. Yes. I was a batman – as I suppose yer remember.

LEAR. I'm sorry. I was thinking about something else. I've written to Cordelia, but she doesn't answer. Yes, there's just the four of us. They moved in when the house was empty, and they've looked after me since I came back. I thought I'd die but they saved me. But tell me about your life. I'd like to know how you've lived and what you've done.

SMALL MAN. O nothin'. Not t' interest your class a person. Not worth tellin'.

LEAR. But you've fought in great wars and helped to make great changes in the world.

SMALL MAN. What?

> THOMAS *comes out of the house and the* SMALL MAN *jumps up.*

O – this your place?

THOMAS. Where've you come from?

SMALL MAN. Well, my wife dies so I was on me own. I says t' meself – travel! See the world while it's still there. New bed every night, a new life every mornin' –

THOMAS. But why are you in that state?

SMALL MAN. Well. (*Sits.*) Yes, why shouldn't I tell yer. I wasn't goin' t' tell yer – the truth upsets people. But you're men of the world. I got beaten up. These thugs, they'd feed their own kids to a guard dog t' keep it quiet –

THOMAS. He's lying –

SMALL MAN. I take an oath – as I stand 'ere –

THOMAS. You're lying!

LEAR. Of course he's lying! Did it take you that long to find out?

THOMAS. Anyone could have sent him! He might be dangerous!

SMALL MAN. No, no, that's not true. Dangerous! (*Half laughs.*) God knows I couldn't 'urt a fly.

THOMAS. Then who are you? Tell me!

SMALL MAN. No! I came t' see 'im, not you!

THOMAS. Who are you?

SMALL MAN. Nobody! I'm from the wall a course – are you stupid? I ran away! I couldn't work. Anyone can see I'm sick. I spit blood. So they put me in a punishment squad. And then the black market . . . (*He stops.*) But if yer can't work they don't feed yer! So I ran. God knows what I was doin'. I must a bin off me 'ead. It's too late now.

THOMAS. But why did you come here?

SMALL MAN. I 'id in the trees but they was everywhere. – What made me what? They're all afraid in the camps so news travels fast. Thass 'ow we 'eard a you.

SUSAN (*off*). It's ready.

SMALL MAN. When I come here I said – say it ain't true, juss talk, an' they give yer up? O Chriss, I didn't know what t' think. Thass why I said yer knew me. You bein' blind I thought –

LEAR. What did you hear in the camp?

SMALL MAN. Yer wan'a get rid a the army an' blow up the wall, an' shut the camps an' send the prisoners home. Yer give money to a deserter.

THOMAS. Did you?

SMALL MAN. An' I was goin' t' die on the wall.

JOHN *comes in.*

JOHN. There's soldiers coming up the hill.

LEAR. Take him in the woods.

THOMAS. Lear! –

LEAR. No! Tell me all that later. Hide him. Warn Susan. He hasn't been here.

> SMALL MAN *whimpers.* THOMAS *hurries with him into the house.*

Sit down. (JOHN *and* LEAR *sit. Pause. He talks to fill the silence, so that they will seem at ease.*) Your young girl will be waiting in the village.

JOHN. Yes. I'm late again. Something always happens, and she gets upset . . .

LEAR. Will you marry her?

JOHN (*listening*). They're coming.

LEAR. Have you asked her? She might not have you.

JOHN. No, not yet.

> *An* OFFICER *and* THREE SOLDIERS (P, Q, *and* R) *come in.*

There's some soldiers here, Lear.

LEAR (*nods*). Is there anything you want? Water or food?

OFFICER. Who else is here?

LEAR. There's a woman in the house and another man somewhere.

OFFICER. Who else?

LEAR. No one.

OFFICER (*to* SOLDIERS). Look round. (SOLDIERS P *and* Q *go into the house. To* JOHN.) Have you seen anyone?

LEAR. He was at work, he's just got back.

SOLDIER R (*offering to go*). Scout round the woods, sir?

OFFICER (*irritated*). You'll never find him in there.

> SUSAN *comes out of the house and stands still.*

(*To* LEAR.) A man was asking for you in the village. Small, dark man.

LEAR. Well, he'll turn up if they told him where I am. I'll let you know.

SOLDIERS P *and* Q *come out of the house.*

SOLDIER P (*shakes his head*). Dead.
OFFICER (*to* LEAR). Very well. This place will be watched in
    future.

The OFFICER *and* THREE SOLDIERS *leave.*

JOHN. They've gone.
LEAR. Go and see them off.

JOHN goes out. SUSAN *goes upstage and calls.*

SUSAN. Tom! (*To* LEAR.) They can't do anything to us. We didn't
    ask him to come. I'll give him some food to take with him. If
    he's caught he can say he stole it.

THOMAS *comes in.* SUSAN *goes to him.*

THOMAS. What happened? What did they say?
LEAR. I don't know. I didn't listen. They were just soldiers. No
    rank.
THOMAS. We must get rid of him quick. If he's caught here now
    we're for it.

BEN, *the young orderly, comes in. He is dirty, dishevelled,
    ragged and breathless. They stare at him.*

BEN. There were soldiers out on the road. I 'ad t' crawl the last bit
    on me 'ands an' knees.

The SMALL MAN *comes in and watches.*

(*Goes to* LEAR.) I looked after you in the cage, sir. They put me
    on the wall for floggin' snout t' cons.
LEAR. Yes. You fed me in prison. You can stay here.
THOMAS. No!
LEAR. He can stay.
THOMAS. But we'll all be responsible. They'll say we encourage
    them! They'll blame us for everything! It's insane!
LEAR. Where else can he go? *You* go if you're afraid!

THOMAS. How can you be so obstinate, how can you be such a
  fool?

BEN (*to* LEAR). Yeh, you ain' some prisoner no one's ever 'eard of,
  they can't mess you about.

LEAR. No, you mustn't say that. I'm not a king. I have no power.
  But you can stay. You're doing no harm. Now I'm hungry, take
  me inside. I'll write to Cordelia again. She means well, she only
  needs someone to make her see sense. Take me in. I came here
  when I was cold and hungry and afraid. I wasn't turned away,
  and I won't turn anyone away. They can eat my food while it
  lasts and when it's gone they can go if they like, but I won't
  send anyone away. That's how I'll end my life. I'll be shut up
  in a grave soon, and till then this door is open. (*He smiles.*)

  LEAR *and the others go towards the house.*

SMALL MAN (*following them. He speaks half to himself*). Thass all
  very well. But yer never seen 'is sort on the wall. We can't let
  everyone in. We 'ave t' act fly.

  The SMALL MAN *follows the others into the house.*

SCENE TWO

Same.

Months later. Many strangers have gathered to listen to LEAR.
THOMAS *leads him out of the house and down to the audience and
turns* LEAR *to face them. As* LEAR *comes down a few* STRANGERS
say 'Good morning' and LEAR *smiles at them and says 'Good
morning'.*

THOMAS *stands at* LEAR's *side and* JOHN *stands a little way back.
The* STRANGERS *watch with respect.*

LEAR (*to the audience*). A man woke up one morning and found
  he'd lost his voice. So he went to look for it, and when he came

to the wood there was the bird who'd stolen it. It was singing beautifully and the man said 'Now I sing so beautifully I shall be rich and famous'. He put the bird in a cage and said 'When I open my mouth wide you must sing'. Then he went to the king and said 'I will sing your majesty's praises'. But when he opened his mouth the bird could only groan and cry because it was in a cage, and the king had the man whipped. The man took the bird home, but his family couldn't stand the bird's groaning and crying and they left him. So in the end the man took the bird back to the wood and let it out of the cage. But the man believed the king had treated him unjustly and he kept saying to himself 'The king's a fool' and as the bird still had the man's voice it kept singing this all over the wood and soon the other birds learned it. The next time the king went hunting he was surprised to hear all the birds singing 'The king's a fool'. He caught the bird who'd started it and pulled out its feathers, broke its wings and nailed it to a branch as a warning to all the other birds. The forest was silent. And just as the bird had the man's voice the man now had the bird's pain. He ran round silently waving his head and stamping his feet, and he was locked up for the rest of his life in a cage.

The STRANGERS *murmur.*

A STRANGER. Tell me, Lear –
THOMAS. Later. He must rest now.

> THOMAS *leads* LEAR *to one side. The* STRANGERS *break up into groups and talk. A few leave.*

I want you to send Ben back to the wall.
LEAR. Why?
THOMAS. Hundreds of people come to hear you now. The government can't let this go on, and they could crush us like that! We need support. We must infiltrate the camps.

> BEN *has been watching intensely. He comes over to them.*

BEN. Has he told you? I'll give myself up. They'll put me in a punishment squad. I'll be beaten and starved and worked like an animal. I may not survive – but at least I'll use what time I've got left. I'll help them to organize and be ready. I can bring them hope. You must give me a message to take –

LEAR. If I saw Christ on his cross I would spit at him.

BEN. What?

LEAR. Take me away.

THOMAS. You haven't listened!

BEN. Listen to us!

LEAR. Take me away!

> THOMAS *leads* LEAR *towards the house. Some of the* STRANGERS *meet him and take him inside.* BEN *and* THOMAS *look at one another in silence.* SUSAN *puts an arm round* THOMAS *to comfort him.*

THOMAS. You look tired.

SUSAN. No.

THOMAS (*sitting down with her*). Don't work too hard.

SUSAN. I'm not.

THOMAS (*presses her*). And don't run round after all these people. They can look after themselves.

SUSAN. O I don't mind them. But when we have our baby –

THOMAS. You don't have to worry about that. They'll all help.

SUSAN. Only it's a small house. Sometimes I'd like to speak to you and there are so many people –

THOMAS. Speak about what? You can always speak to me.

SUSAN. O I don't know. I meant . . . (*She is silent.*)

THOMAS (*thinking about* LEAR. *After a slight pause*). We talk to people but we don't really help them. We shouldn't let them come here if that's all we can do. It's dangerous to tell the truth, truth without power is always dangerous. And we *should* fight! Freedom's not an idea, it's a passion! If you haven't got it you fight like a fish out of water fighting for air!

> *The* STRANGERS *who left hurry on quickly.*

STRANGERS (*quietly and intensely*). Soldiers. Soldiers.

> THOMAS *stands.*

THOMAS. What is it?

> *The* OLD COUNCILLOR, *an* OFFICER *and* SOLDIERS P, Q *and* R *come on.*

OFFICER (*reads from a form*). Rossman – (BEN *comes forward.*) – and – (*He points at the* SMALL MAN *as he tries to slip away.*) – grab him – (SOLDIERS P *and* Q *stop the* SMALL MAN.) – Jones –

SMALL MAN. Thass not me! I'm Simpson!

OFFICER. – I'm taking you into custody as absentees from your work camps.

> LEAR *is led from the house. He stands on the steps surrounded by* STRANGERS.

LEAR. Who is it? What d'you want?

OFFICER. You're harbouring deserters.

LEAR. I don't ask my friends who they are.

BEN. Let them take me!

SOLDIER R. Shut it!

OFFICER. I'm returning them under guard to the area military commandant.

SMALL MAN (*tries to go to* LEAR *but the* SOLDIERS *stop him*). For God's sake what d'you want me for? Yer can see I'm ill! What work can I do? I'm in everyone's way. For god's sake leave me alone.

OFFICER. You're not going back to work. Certain economic offences have been made capital with retrospective effect. You were found guilty of dealing on the unauthorized market. The revised sentence is mandatory.

SMALL MAN (*bewildered*). I don't understand that.

OFFICER. You're a social liability. You're going back to be hanged.

SMALL MAN (*vaguely*). Yer can't . . . I've already been dealt with. It's on me records, sir. I don't understand.

LEAR. Take me to him. (LEAR *is led to the* OFFICER. *He puts his hand on the* OFFICER's *arm. Quietly.*) You're a soldier, how many deaths are on your conscience? Don't burden yourself with two more. Go back and say you can't find them.

COUNCILLOR. Lear, every word you say is treason.

LEAR. Who's that? Who's there?

COUNCILLOR. I was your minister –

LEAR. Yes – I know you!

COUNCILLOR. Out of respect for your age and sufferings Cordelia has tolerated your activities, but now they must stop. In future you will not speak in public or involve yourself in any public affairs. Your visitors will be vetted by the area military authorities. All these people must go. The government will appoint a man and woman to look after you. You will live in decent quietness, as a man of your years should.

LEAR. Are you in their new government?

COUNCILLOR. Like many of my colleagues I gave the new undertaking of loyalty. I've always tried to serve people. I see that as my chief duty. If we abandon the administration there'd be chaos.

LEAR. Yes, yes – but you won't hang this man for money?

SMALL MAN. The records must be wrong . . . That's it!

OFFICER. Take him down to the road.

SMALL MAN (*bewildered. Whimpers*). No.

LEAR (*to* COUNCILLOR). Stop them.

COUNCILLOR. It isn't my concern at all. I came to speak to *you*.

LEAR. I see. Savages have taken my power. You commit crimes and call them the law! The giant must stand on his toes to prove he's tall! – No, I'm wrong to shout at you, you have so much to do, things to put right, all my mistakes, I understand all that . . . But he's a little swindler! A petty swindler! Think of the crimes you commit every day in your office, day after day till it's just routine, think of the waste and misery of that!

COUNCILLOR. I was sent to talk to you as an old friend, not to be insulted, Lear. He'll be taken back to the wall and hanged. And – as you are interested in my views – I think he should be.

LEAR. O I know what you think! Whatever's trite and vulgar and hard and shallow and cruel, with no mercy or sympathy – that's what you think, and you're proud of it! You good, decent, honest, upright, lawful men who believe in order – when the last man dies, you will have killed him! I have lived with murderers and thugs, there are limits to their greed and violence, but you decent, honest men devour the earth!

SOLDIERS P *and* Q *start to take the* SMALL MAN *out.*

SMALL MAN. No – stop them!

LEAR. There's nothing I can do! The government's mad. The law's mad.

SMALL MAN (*throws himself at* LEAR). Then why did yer let me come 'ere? O God, I know I'm bad sometimes and I don't deserve to – O God, please!

LEAR. There's nothing I can do!

SMALL MAN. Then I should a stayed an' be shot like a dog. I lived like a dog, what did it matter? It'd be finished now. Why've I suffered all this?

The SMALL MAN *is taken out crying. The* OFFICER, OLD COUNCILLOR, BEN *and* SOLDIERS *go with him.* LEAR *starts to push the* STRANGERS *out.*

LEAR. Send them away!

JOHN. You'll fall!

LEAR (*stumbling up and down. Flailing with his stick*). Send them away! The government's given its orders. Power has spoken. Get out! What are you doing here? What have I been telling you? There's nothing to learn here! I'm a fool! A fool! Get out!

SUSAN (*turning away*). O god.

LEAR. Send them away! Throw them out!

THOMAS. They're going. (*He talks as quietly as he can to the* STRANGERS.) Wait in the village. I'll talk to him.

LEAR. Get out! Get out! I said get rid of them!

The STRANGERS *go.* LEAR, SUSAN, THOMAS *and* JOHN *are left.*

THOMAS. They've gone.

LEAR. Get out! All of you! Leave me alone!

THOMAS. No! I must know what to tell them. We're not backing out now.

LEAR. O go away! Go! Go! Go! Who is this stupid man who keeps talking to me?

JOHN (*pulls* THOMAS). Come on.

THOMAS. Sit! I'll go if you sit!

LEAR. O go . . . Go.

LEAR *sits.* THOMAS, JOHN *and* SUSAN *go into the house.*

What can I do? I left my prison, pulled it down, broke the key, and still I'm a prisoner. I hit my head against a wall all the time. There's a wall everywhere. I'm buried alive in a wall. Does this suffering and misery last for ever? Do we work to build ruins, waste all these lives to make a desert no one could live in? There's no one to explain it to me, no one I can go to for justice. I'm old, I should know how to live by now, but I know nothing, I can do nothing, I am nothing.

The GHOST *comes in. It is thinner, shrunk, a livid white.*

GHOST. Look at my hands! They're like claws. See how thin I am.

LEAR. Yes, you. Go with the rest. Get out. It's finished. There's nothing here now, nothing. Nothing's left.

GHOST. There's too much. Send these people away. Let them learn to bear their own sufferings. No, that hurts too much. That's what you can't bear: they suffer and no one can give them justice.

LEAR. Every night my life is laid waste by a cry. I go out in the dark but I never find who's there. How do most men live? They're hungry and no one feeds them, so they call for help and

no one comes. And when their hunger's worse they scream –
and jackals and wolves come to tear them to pieces.

GHOST. Yes. That's the world you have to learn to live in. Learn
it! Let me poison the well.

LEAR. Why?

GHOST. Then no one can live here, they'll have to leave you alone.
There's a spring hidden in the wood. I'll take you there every
day to drink. Lie down. Look how tired you are. Lie down.

> LEAR *lies down.*

Cordelia will come tomorrow and you can tell her you know
how to keep silent at last.

> *It's dark.* LEAR *sleeps on the bench.* JOHN *comes out of the
> house with a bundle. He crosses the stage.* SUSAN *comes to the
> door. He sees her and stops.*

SUSAN. Why are you taking your things?

JOHN. Come with me.

SUSAN. No.

JOHN. I love you. Your husband doesn't any more. He's full of
Lear.

SUSAN (*angrily*). He does love me!

JOHN. I see. (*Slight pause.*) I was used to saying nothing, but you
came out so I told you. How beautiful you are. There's nothing
to say, you know all about me. I'll wait in the village. If you
don't come I'll marry the girl down there. But I'll wait a few
days, or I'll always be sorry.

> JOHN *goes.* SUSAN *sits on the steps and starts to cry, quietly and
> methodically.* THOMAS *comes in the doorway behind her.*

THOMAS. Stop crying.

SUSAN. Take me away.

THOMAS. I can't leave him now. It'd be cruel.

SUSAN (*still crying*). I know he's mad. You shouldn't keep me
here when I'm like this.

THOMAS (*calmly and quietly*). There's been enough tears for one
day. Stop crying and come inside.

> THOMAS *goes back into the house.* SUSAN *stops crying and
> follows him in.*

SCENE THREE

Woods.

LEAR *is alone. He wears outdoor clothes. He gropes on his hands and
knees. Off, the pigs start to squeal angrily.* LEAR *stands. The*
GHOST *comes in. Its flesh has dried up, its hair is matted, its
face is like a seashell, the eyes are full of terror.*

GHOST. I frighten the pigs. They run when they see me.

LEAR. I was collecting acorns for them. (*He stands.*)

GHOST. The soldiers are moving into the village. They're sealing
you off. Will you send the people away?

LEAR. No.

GHOST. I thought you'd forget all this: crowds, wars, arguments.
. . . We could have been happy living here. I used to be happy.
I'd have led you about and watched you grow old, your beauti-
ful old age . . .

LEAR. We buried your body here. And Warrington's. It's beautiful
under the trees. I thought I might think of something to tell
Cordelia out here. I don't know . . . They're coming to bury me
and I'm still asking how to live. Can you hear the wind?

GHOST. No. My mind goes. You hear very well when you're
blind.

LEAR. Yes.

GHOST. Can you hear an owl on the hill?

LEAR. Yes.

GHOST. But not the fox.

LEAR. No.

GHOST. No. (*He starts to cry.*)

LEAR (*listens to him crying*). Why?

GHOST. Because I'm dead. I knew how to live. You'll never know. It was so easy, I had everything I wanted here. I was afraid sometimes, like sheep are, but it never haunted me, it would go . . . Now I'm dead I'm afraid of death. I'm wasting away, my mind doesn't work . . . I go away somewhere and suddenly I find myself standing by the house or out in the fields . . . It happens more now . . .

CORDELIA *and the* CARPENTER *come in.*

CORDELIA. Lear. (*She holds* LEAR's *hand for a moment.*) I've brought my husband.

LEAR. You've been to the house? Did it upset you?

CORDELIA. No. I wanted to see it.

LEAR. Are you well?

CORDELIA. Yes. And you? D'you need anything?

LEAR. No.

CORDELIA. I came because the cabinet wants you to be tried. There could only be one sentence. Your daughters were killed. And it's clear there's no real difference between you and them.

LEAR. None.

CORDELIA. You were here when they killed my husband. I watched them kill him. I covered my face with my hands, but my fingers opened so I watched. I watched them rape me, and John kill them, and my child miscarry. I didn't miss anything. I watched and I said we won't be at the mercy of brutes anymore, we'll live a new life and help one another. The government's creating that new life – you must stop speaking against us.

LEAR. Stop people listening.

CORDELIA. I can't. You say what they want to hear.

LEAR. If that's true – if only some of them want to hear – I must speak.

CORDELIA. Yes, you sound like the voice of my conscience. But if you listened to everything your conscience told you you'd go mad. You'd never get anything done – and there's a lot to do, some of it very hard.

GHOST. Tell her I'm here. Make her talk about me.

LEAR. Don't build the wall.

CORDELIA. We must.

LEAR. Then nothing's changed! A revolution must at least reform!

CORDELIA. Everything *else* is changed!

LEAR. Not if you keep the wall! Pull it down!

CORDELIA. We'd be attacked by our enemies!

LEAR. The wall will destroy you. It's already doing it. How can I make you see?

GHOST. Tell her I'm here. Tell her.

CARPENTER. We came to talk to you, not listen. My wife wants to tell you something.

LEAR. She came like the rest! And she'll listen like the rest! I didn't go out of my way to make trouble. But I will not be quiet when people come here. And if you stop them – that would be easy! – they'll know I'm here or was here *once*! I've suffered so much, I made all the mistakes in the world and I pay for each of them. I cannot be forgotten. I am in their minds. To kill me you must kill them all. Yes, that's who I am. Listen, Cordelia. You have two enemies, lies *and* the truth. You sacrifice truth to destroy lies, and you sacrifice life to destroy death. It isn't sane. You squeeze a stone till your hand bleeds and call that a miracle. I'm old, but I'm as weak and clumsy as a child, too heavy for my legs. But I've learned this, and you must learn it or you'll die. Listen, Cordelia. If a god had made the world, might would always be right, that would be so wise, we'd be spared so much suffering. But we made the world – out of our smallness and weakness. Our lives are awkward and fragile and we have only one thing to keep us sane: pity, and the man without pity is mad.

The GHOST *starts to cry as* CORDELIA *speaks.*

CORDELIA. You only understand self-pity. We must go back, the government's waiting. There are things you haven't been told. We have other opponents, more ruthless than you. In this situation a good government acts strongly. I knew you wouldn't co-operate, but I wanted to come and tell you this before we put you on trial: we'll make the society you only dream of.

LEAR. It's strange that you should have me killed, Cordelia, but it's obvious you would. How simple! Your law always does more harm than crime, and your morality is a form of violence.

CORDELIA (*to* CARPENTER). The sooner it's finished now the better. Call a cabinet for the morning.

CORDELIA *and the* CARPENTER *go out.*

GHOST. Why didn't you tell her I was here? She wanted to talk about me. She couldn't forget me. I made love to her in that house night after night, and on this grass. Look at me now! I've turned into *this* – I can't even touch her!

LEAR. Where are you going?

GHOST. I can watch her go.

The GHOST *goes out.* THOMAS *and* SUSAN *come on. They have dressed up a little because of the visitors.*

THOMAS. We waited till they went. Shall I take you back?

LEAR. Listen, I must talk to you. I'm going on a journey and Susan will lead me.

THOMAS. Yes, go into hiding! Don't let them get their filthy hands on you.

LEAR. Tomorrow morning we'll get up and have breakfast together and you'll go to work, but Susan will stay with me. She may not be back tomorrow evening, but she'll be back soon, I promise you. You're fond of me and I've been happy with you. I'm lucky. Now I have only one more wish – to live till I'm much older and become as cunning as the fox, who knows how to live. *Then* I could teach you.

Off, distant squealing of angry pigs, further off than at the end of Act One, Scene Seven.

THOMAS. The pigs!
SUSAN. What is it?

SUSAN and THOMAS run off. LEAR stands by himself.

THOMAS (*off*). They've gone mad!
SUSAN (*off*). Quick!
THOMAS (*off*). That way!
SUSAN (*off*). Look out!
THOMAS (*off*). Berserk! Wup-wup-wup-wup-wup-wup-wup!
SUSAN (*off*). Wup-wup-wup! Mad!

The GHOST stumbles in. It is covered with blood. The pig squeals slowly die out. A few more isolated calls of 'wup'.

GHOST. The pigs! I'm torn! They gored me! Help me, help me! I'll die!
LEAR (*holds him*). I can't!
GHOST. Lear! Hold me!
LEAR. No, too late! It's far too late! You were killed long ago! You must die! I love you, I'll always remember you, but I can't help you. Die, for your own sake die!
GHOST. O Lear, I am dead!

The GHOST's head falls back. It is dead. It drops at LEAR's feet. The calls and pig squeals stop.

LEAR. I see my life, a black tree by a pool. The branches are covered with tears. The tears are shining with light. The wind blows the tears in the sky. And my tears fall down on me.

SCENE FOUR

The wall.
A steep earth bank. A stack of tools at the bottom of the bank. Clear
daylight. SUSAN *leads* LEAR *on. He has no stick.*

SUSAN. This is the wall.
LEAR. Where are the tools?
SUSAN. On the ground in front of you.
LEAR. You were angry with me.
SUSAN. I was, but I'm not now.
LEAR (*kisses her*). Goodbye. Go back alone.
SUSAN. I can't! Who'll look after you. My husband would be
  angry.
LEAR. No. He'll understand now.

> SUSAN *goes out.* LEAR *goes to the tools. He finds a shovel.*

A shovel. (*He climbs the wall.*) It's built to last. So steep, and my
breath's short. (*He reaches the top.*) The wind's cold, I must be
quick. (*He digs the shovel in.*) Work soon warms you up.

> *He throws a shovel of earth down the side and digs the shovel in*
> *again. A* BOY *comes on and stares at* LEAR. LEAR *throws*
> *another shovel of earth down. The* BOY *goes out in the direction*
> *he came.*

This will be three. (*He digs the shovel in again.*) The tool's got
no edge. No one cares for it.

> *A group of* WORKERS *come on and stare at* LEAR. *He leaves the*
> *shovel stuck in the earth. He takes off his coat and folds it neatly.*
> *A junior officer comes in. It is the* FARMER'S SON. *He watches.*
> LEAR *lays his folded coat on the ground and turns back to the*
> *shovel.*

FARMER'S SON. Oi, I know yoo, boy. What yoo up to now?

The FARMER'S SON *aims his pistol.*

LEAR (*spits on his hand and grips the shovel*). I'm not as fit as I was. I can still make my mark.

LEAR *digs the shovel into the earth. The* FARMER'S SON *fires.* LEAR *is killed instantly. He falls down the wall. The shovel stays upright in the earth. Some of the* WORKERS *move toward the body with curiosity.*

FARMER'S SON. Leave that. They'll pick en up. Off now.

The WORKERS *go quickly and orderly. One of them looks back. The* FARMER'S SON *shepherds them off, and marches off after them.* LEAR'*s body is left alone on stage.*

END

Notes

Act I

Scene One

1 *tarpaulin* — a waterproof cloth or sheet of heavy material, generally used out-of-doors to provide protection against rain or damp ground.

1 *yer* — a dialect form of 'you'.

1 *'andin' in 'is pick t' stores* — returning his pick to the place officially responsible for the provision and storage of tools and equipment (dialect).

1 *Bodice* — (pronounced: Boddiss) literally, a woman's garment; perhaps intended to suggest Boadicea, warrior queen killed in rebellion against the Romans in 61 A.D. Not common as a name.

2 *Fontanelle* — literally, the soft spot on an infant's skull. Not common as a name.

2 *a flogging crime* — a fault for which the punishment is to be whipped.

3 *scuttle* — run in a hurried, insect-like manner, as if to escape danger and detection.

3 *spring traps* — devices made of metal, with 'jaws' designed to snap shut and trap any animal which releases the spring-mechanism. Man-traps were used in the past by landowners to discourage poachers on their estates, but their use is now illegal.

3 *Court martial him* — try his case before a military tribunal.

3 *A drumhead trial* — a summary or improvised trial, held immediately when and where a breach of military discipline occurs so that the offender can be dealt with promptly and sometimes harshly to provide a warning to others.

3 *roll calls* — the reading out of a list of names to discover those people missing from a group.

3 *in the field* — on the battlefield, by military action.

4 *hand in glove* — working in close partnership.

4 *an old spinster* — an elderly, unmarried woman. The term 'old maidish', or 'spinsterish' is sometimes applied to men considered to be timid, easily shocked, and ineffective.

6   *Behind my back* — secretly, without my knowledge.

6   *I can tell a man from his expression* — I can see a man's character by looking at his face.

6   *like wolves in a fold* — like wolves amongst sheep, they will be brutal and destructive.

6   *out of hand* — out of all reasonable proportion, uncontrolled, intemperate.

6   *My feet are wringing* — my feet are soaking wet.

7   *They are my sheep* — they are in my care, under my protection. The phrase has a Biblical reference to the idea of Christ as the Good Shepherd, prepared to search tirelessly to find any one of his sheep that might be lost.

7   *it would come to this* — this would be the result.

8   *caught out* — taken by surprise, unprepared.

8   *keep in with him* — remain in favour, retain his good opinion.

Scene Two

8   *a saluting stand* — a platform from which a high-ranking official can salute his troops as they pass in review before him.

8   *my right flank* — the divisions of soldiers positioned on the far right of an army's battle-formation.

9   *Greetings to my glorious ninth* — Julius Caesar's salute to his most effective and favoured legion, the Ninth. Lear thus places himself within a great military tradition.

9   *fall into their hands* — become their prisoner.

9   *This fry* — this insignificant and inexperienced group of rebels. The reference is more usually to 'small fry'.

Scene Three

10   *set in his ways* — become incapable of changing his behaviour, having fixed ideas and responses.

10   *work myself off* — find sexual relief through masturbation (colloquial).

10   *making do* — having to accept something second-rate, unsatisfactory.

10   *to get his little paddle in* — to have sexual intercourse (vulgar).

11   *mawl* — cry like a cat.

11   *to raise his standard* — to perform satisfactorily as a lover. The *double entendre* is appropriately contained within a military expression usually applied to a general's or king's gathering of an army to fight for his cause behind his flag or standard.

Scene Four

11 *They wan'a* — they want to, they should (dialect).

11 *Watered 'im* — given him a drink of water.

12 *allow for* — take into consideration when making plans.

13 *Yessam* — Yes, madam (dialect).

13 *flicks* — makes a small, abrupt movement, nods in a particular direction.

13 *Thass sometimes arst for* — that is sometimes asked for (dialect).

13 *give a 'and t' flay a man* — helped to strip the skin off a man. A punishment used by the medieval church.

13 *Wind and piss* — full of offensive threats but finally ineffective (vulgar). 'Piss' is a vulgar term for urine.

13 *thass juss for a start* — that is just a first step (dialect).

13 *Get it goin' and see 'ow it goes from there* — start the process off and then see what further action suggests itself.

13 *turn yer inside out* — Bond has said this was meant literally; it means that the victim's innards would be pulled to the outside.

14 *'e wants it the 'ard way* — he is prepared to endure more pain than is necessary in his effort to behave like an officer-gentleman and not show his suffering.

14 *puttin' on the officer class* — behaving as he imagines an officer should, that is, bravely.

14 *Don't pull yer pips on me, laddie* — don't try to impress me with your superior rank (colloquial). 'Laddie' simply indicates the soldier's attitude of scornful assertiveness. 'Pips' refer to the metal studs worn on some military uniforms to signify rank.

14 *Lay off* — stop doing that, don't interfere (colloquial).

14 *One plain, two pearl* — a very common sequence of knitting stitches.

14 *Thass a bit 'eavy* — contains two ideas: that Warrington is too heavy for the soldier to lift without assistance; and that Fontanelle's request goes beyond reasonable bounds.

14 *Thass boney-fidey sufferin'* — that is genuine suffering (dialect).

15 *'E's a poor ol' gent, lonely ol' bugger* — he's a pathetic old man, with no friends. 'Bugger' is used as a term of general abuse, sometimes mildly affectionate.

15 *I'd die to listen* — I want more than anything else to listen.

15 *It's my duty to inform you* — Bodice is here using the formal language of the police and court officials.

15 *jog these in and out* — push with a jerk. The word 'jog' is generally used to describe a slight and accidental bumping into something, or a gentle activity, so is disturbing in this context. This

feeling is heightened by her then making the kind of nonsense
noises used to entertain babies, usually in a sing-song voice, or
suggesting carefree enjoyment of some slight pleasure.

15 *You old vulture* — an insulting reference to Fontanelle's
macabre delight in the pain and probable death of others.

16 *let my knitting run* — allowed the stitches to become
unravelled.

16 *dilly-dally* — idly waste time.

16 *see what my husband's up to* — find out what my husband is
doing that I might have cause to object to.

16 *offal* — means both garbage, such as scraps of unwanted and
probably rotten food, and those parts cut off from the carcass of
an animal to be sold for food.

16 *t'morra* — a dialect corruption of 'tomorrow'.

16 *less 'ave yer* — let's get you to your feet and on your way
(dialect).

Scene Five

16 *Put yourself in their hands* — allow them to take charge of
you, guide you.

17 *had plastic surgery* — work carried out by a surgeon, in this
case very clumsily, to restore damage done to a person's skin and
visible tissues. Plastic surgery is also sometimes performed for
cosmetic reasons, to improve a person's features.

Scene Six

18 *struck a well* — while digging, discovered a natural source of
water, with a man-made shaft sunk to make the water more easily
accessible.

19 *grub round* — search for food on or in the ground.

19 *out of habit* — because it was what she did so often that it had
become almost routine, not necessarily prompted by any specific
cause of sorrow.

20 *she's carrying* — she's pregnant.

Scene Seven

22 *Swill bucket* — a bucket which had contained liquid food for
the pigs.

23 *shut the pigs up* — this phrase contains two ideas: 'put the pigs
into a pen or pig-sty' and 'make them quiet'.

24 *hanging round* — staying close by without having any specific
reason to do so.

26 *a bad match* — not suitable for each other as marriage-partners.

27 *I'm carrying* — (see note on p.20).

27 *hire myself to* — agree to work for payment. More usually 'to hire' describes the payment of a fee for the temporary use or possession of property, so Lear's choice of phrase conveys his feeling that to become a paid labourer would undermine his human dignity.

27 *at everyone's call* — required to come and go, fetch and carry, at the command of people in general.

27 *get rid of* — firmly send away, dispose of.

28 *Turn it over inside* — search the inside of the house thoroughly, even if it means creating mess and disorder.

28 *'Oo else yer got knockin' around?'* — who else is likely to be here? (Dialect).

28 *Shouldn't lie your age* — You are too old to be telling lies (dialect).

28 *yer knowd* — you knew (dialect).

28 *yer must a 'ad some one t' put in that class* — there must have been someone here to make you pregnant (dialect).

28 *a bin 'im* — have been him (dialect).

28 *'Ed'd 'ave t'use a carrot* — a vulgar reference to the fact that Lear was obviously too old to impregnate the woman himself.

28 *dirty ol' toe rag* — filthy, old beggar (dialect).

28 *a nice little lay* — a sexually attractive young woman (vulgar).

30 *An' run 'im down t' truck* — march him quickly down to the truck.

30 *jammy bastard* — someone who seems to get lighter or more enjoyable work than others (vulgar).

31 *Shut it* — Be quiet (colloquial).

31 *An' I'll 'ave 'er reekin' a pig blood* — when I have sexual intercourse with her I'll be smelling of pigs' blood (dialect).

31 *cold chisel* — a tool designed to cut through masonry.

31 *a fraction* — a few seconds.

Act II

Scene One

32 *have his life* — have him killed.

32 *a safe prison* — there is an ironic reversal here of the usual idea that a 'safe' or maximum security prison is to protect society from further crimes by locking up the criminals; here the prison is to keep Lear 'safe' from his daughters.

32 *Family sentiment doesn't cloud our judgement* — our ability to think clearly is not affected by any feelings we may have towards our father. There is significant irony in the statement.

32 *rattle on* — talk at length and to no real purpose.

33 *Honours list* — an announcement, generally issued formally by the Head of State, naming those to be given official recognition of their services to the nation or to their local community.

33 *the late king* — 'late' here means 'one time' or 'former', but sinisterly conveys the more familiar sense of 'recently dead', and thus indicates that Lear's death is imminent and certain enough to be spoken of as an accomplished fact.

34 *Take the oath first* — English law requires a witness in court to swear an oath affirming that what he is about to say will be entirely and comprehensively true. Thus a witness giving false testimony becomes guilty of the punishable offence of perjury.

35 *You have no right to sit there* — Lear's response echoes the assertion made by England's Charles I that the court summoned by Parliament, under the leadership of Oliver Cromwell, had no constitutional or legally valid right to try him, their king. He was, nonetheless, condemned to death and beheaded in 1649.

35 *its snout* — its nose and mouth.

36 *adjourned* — suspended for a while, perhaps until the following day.

36 *Keep him on a tighter leash* — keep him more firmly under control, allow him less freedom.

36 *root it out* — uncover and deal decisively with it.

36 *Meet it head on* — take the initiative in dealing with danger, refuse to run away.

36 *riffraff* — unimpressive assortment of disreputable, unruly people.

36 *goes to her head* — makes her act extravagantly or over-ambitiously.

36 *The head must be squeezed* — Bodice changes the sense of 'head' now to mean the blister on top of an infected spot which can be squeezed to release the pus.

36 *her days are numbered* — her death is already certain and imminent.

37 *purged* — cleared of any treacherous or hostile elements.

Scene Two

37 *Cross laddie 'ere off* — cross this fellow's name off the list (dialect).

38 *that terrible bell* — this bell seems to be both one tolled to mark a funeral and (see p.42) a bell rung to indicate tea-time.

39 *Don't 'ang it out, grandad* — Don't take so long, old man (colloquial).

39 *the empties* − the dirty plates and glasses (usually applied to the glasses emptied by drinkers in a bar).

39 *I ain't the chef, I'm only the 'ead waiter* − I didn't cook the food; I'm just responsible for serving it. There is both humour and pathos in the orderly's use of Cockney chattiness in these circumstances.

40 *an' take it all in* − and pay attention to everything so that you'll remember it.

40 *Corp* − abbreviated form of 'Corporal', title of a non-commissioned officer in the British Army, ranked just below a sergeant.

40 *Yer skip the personal* − You don't have to search the prisoners' bodies.

40 *When yer off?* − When are you going away? (Dialect).

40 *Tmorra. Least it's out a this 'ole* − Tomorrow. At least it will mean leaving this terrible place (dialect).

41 *Nignogs* − a general term of abuse, most frequently applied to foreigners by intolerant Englishmen (slang). Bond uses it to refer to new recruits, to denote their incompetence − with no racial connotations.

41 *yer know yer own stomach* − you know whether you need to eat or not.

41 *I ain' on the staff* − I'm not one of the officials here. He is evidently one of the prisoners trusted to perform menial tasks.

41 *every crime in the book* − every crime described either in the book of sins listed to assist some Christians make their confession to a priest, or in a book of law, or − more vaguely − a book of rules of some sort (colloquial).

41 *Juss t' put me mind t'rest* − just to stop me worrying (dialect).

42 *The customer knows what 'e wants* − a variation on the commercial cliché that 'the customer is always right', as if Lear were in a restaurant rather than a prison.

Scene Three

42 *Rebel field post* − a position near the battlefield where the rebels give emergency treatment to their wounded and gather to plan immediate tactics.

43 *spuds* − potatoes (slang).

43 *US* − abbreviated form of 'useless'.

43 *These fields are China t'me* − these fields are as strange and unfamiliar to me as parts of China would be (colloquial).

44 *They used t' be regular* − we could depend upon regular supplies of arms, equipment and food.

44 *a yourn* − of yours (dialect).

44 *Not that I'm knockin' your lads* − not that I am trying to belittle or insult your soldiers (colloquial).

44 *if yer like t' look at it* — if you like to think of it this way
(dialect).

44 *in the sticks* — in the country, far from centres of political
and cultural life.

44 *'Ello, we goin' then?* — Hello, are we setting off now? He
seems unaware that he is being taken off to be shot.

Scene Four

46 *slumped forward* — bent over limply, in a completely relaxed
manner.

46 *the only moral institution* — the only organisation either
committed to the preservation of moral standards in society or
being in itself concerned to act morally. It is ironic that this should
be said about spies.

46 *slobbering* — being absurdly and unattractively sentimental in
displaying affection, particularly physical affection.

46 *to sleep with* — go to bed with as a lover.

47 *to leave open* — to leave undecided. 'Closed' implies that the
matter has been dealt with once and for all, an irreversible decision
having been carried through.

47 *plainclothes spies* — spies not wearing any kind of recognisable
uniform.

48 *I'm superstitious, they'll bring us bad luck* — I have an
irrational but powerful fear of doing anything to bring us ill
fortune. Fontanelle's wish to quiet her fear by burning the dukes is
an echo of the historical response to those felt to be witches or in
league with the devil.

48 *bullies* — tries to dominate, force her will on. The term is most
commonly applied to schoolchildren who unkindly take advantage
of those weaker than themselves.

48 *the map's my straitjacket* — I am completely restricted in my
decisions by the need to move my armies strategically from one
point of conflict to the next. Bodice's use of this image to describe
her lack of real power foreshadows Lear's actual loss of freedom in
a straitjacket when he is blinded (p.63).

48 *not reflectively* — not merely interested in thinking (quietly)
about it. She is actively thinking, analysing and working out her
situation.

Scene Five

49 *gagged* — a cloth tied around his face to prevent him from
speaking.

49 *bloody* – an unspecific expression of disgust, like 'blasted'.

49 *Hup Hup!* – Get up and move! It is associated specifically with shouted military commands.

49 *'E knows when 'e's 'ad enough* – he knows when he can do no more, go no further (dialect).

49 *We're 'eadin' back the way we come* – we are retracing our steps (dialect).

49 *Go an'ave a little reccy* – go and take a look around here, reconnoitre (colloquial).

49 *You're good at directions* – you are good at finding your way around, you've got a good sense of direction.

50 *They must a issued this for the Crimea* – they must have handed out this map to soldiers in the Crimean War (1853-1856). In other words, it is out of date and probably even relates to a different area of action. The historical reference is not so much anachronistic as one example of Bond's method of making the play's action free from the restrictions of a set time and place.

50 *I tol' yer t' wrap it* – I told you to stay silent (dialect).

50 *Oi wass your game!* – Hey! What are you trying to do (dialect)!

50 *Wass up?* – What's the matter (colloquial)?

50 *Any more out a you and yer'll look through a 'ole in yer 'ead* – if you cause any more trouble, I'll shoot you in the head (dialect).

50 *I got the enemy breathin' up me arse* – the enemy is very close behind us (vulgarly colloquial).

50 *I ain' messin' about with you* – so I'm not wasting time on you, I mean it (colloquial).

50 *these darlin's* – 'darlings' is used mockingly to describe the prisoners.

51 *I ain' cartin' this garbage round* – I'm not taking on the responsibility and bother of marching these worthless prisoners around (dialect).

51 *Reckon 'e's scarpered?* – do you think he's run away? (Dialect)

51 *Nah* – No.

51 *'Oo unplugged 'is gob?* – who took his gag off so he could talk? (Dialect)

51 *'Ark at it* – listen to that (dialect).

51 *bloody 'ush!* – be quiet. 'Bloody' is used to convey urgency and emphasis.

52 *stow it, grandad* – I told you to be quiet, old man (dialect).

53 *My hands are white* – I am not guilty of any crime.

53 *Don't know any of 'em from Adam* — I've no idea who any of them are.

Scene Six
54 *got rid of the undesirables* — killed all those thought to be dangerous or corrupt.
54 *grub* — food (colloquial).
55 *should a bin out* — should have been released (dialect).
55 *jostling* — pushing and shoving.
56 *It's on standin' orders* — it's part of the official list of duties to be carried out regularly, until new instructions are issued.
56 *Get fell in sharp* — Get into an orderly line quickly (army jargon).
56 *politicals* — political prisoners. They are, therefore, neither soldiers being disciplined nor common criminals.
56 *transferees* — men to be moved from one place to another (a coinage).
56 *Throw their muck anywhere* — they drop their rubbish all over the place.
56 *put a foot right* — do the correct thing.
57 *open . . . closed* — (see note on p. 47).
58 *trestle table* — a table made of boards supported on hinged wooden frames which can be folded up to allow easy storage and carrying.
58 *little autopsy* — a brief, not very thorough examination of the body to establish cause of death.
59 *making a few incisions* — cutting the body open in a few places. Nothing more than a number of such surgical wounds on the body is required by this military regime as evidence of the correct procedures having been performed.
59 *the beast* — the savage, ravening monster that Lear felt his daughter to have been.
59 *like a lion and a lamb and a child* — this is a reference to a passage in the Old Testament picturing an idyllic, harmonious world of nature on God's holy mountain (*Isaiah* 11:6-9).
60 *acted for the best* — did what we believed to be right in the circumstances.
60 *organs* — for example, the heart and lungs.
60 *viscera* — for example, the intestines.
60 *Her blood is on my hands* — not only is this literally true, but Lear also uses the words figuratively to convey his feelings of guilt. (Compare with his claim to have white hands. p. 53.)

61 *show you minutes* — show you the records made of discussions and decisions in committee meetings.

61 *culpable by association* — a legal-sounding phrase meaning that she is guilty or deserves blame only because she was linked in some way with the real offenders.

61 *You have no right!* — (see note on p. 35).

61 *writhes away* — twists away in terror, moving like an anguished snake.

61 *pinion* — hold down firmly.

62 *Blimey* — colloquial exclamation of shock or surprise, originally 'gor blimey' (God blind me).

62 *politically ineffective* — the phrase suggests two ideas: that Lear can be left in such a state that he will be incapable of further political activity; and that he can be disabled in a 'politic' way, in other words, discreetly and without causing public outrage.

62 *Thass only a dose a rabbies* — that's only going to give you a bout of rabies. In other words, being bitten by Bodice is like being bitten by a mad, infected dog.

63 *a straitjacket* — a garment made of strong canvas material, used for restraining the violently insane.

63 *regalia* — the emblems or symbols of royalty.

63 *perfected on dogs* — completed the design satisfactorily by experimenting on dogs.

63 *a scouting gadget* — a tool used by boy scouts. This is startling in this context since boy scouts are supposed to be committed to doing humane and socially useful things, in the tradition of Lord Baden-Powell, founder of the scouting movement. It is also a comic cliché that scouts carry round with them an assortment of useful implements so as to be prepared for any emergency, particularly a hooked tool for, it is said, taking stones out of horses' hooves.

64 *'E'll 'ave the 'hole bloody place up* — he'll rouse everybody.

64 *O lor* — Oh Lord (dialect), indicating alarm.

Scene Seven

The farmer, his wife and son speak in the dialect of country people from the East Anglian region of England. Most characteristic is the lengthening of 'o' into 'oo', the use of 'ont' to mean 'have not', and the use of 'en' for 'him'.

65 *Don't fret* — don't upset yourself.

65 *in the scrub* — amongst these small bushes.

65 *We ont got no bait for yoo* — we've got no food to spare for you (dialect).

65 *Rare land* — exceptionally fertile.

65 *count a* — because (dialect).

65 *We'd best move sharp* — we had better go quickly (dialect).

66 *We can't bait en an' dress en' n' more* — we can no longer manage to feed and clothe him (dialect).

66 *T'ent time t' natter* — there's no time now for idle talk (dialect).

66 *toppled over* — fallen as if unbalanced by the weight of his head. One can also speak of a king being 'toppled' from his throne, so the woman's choice of word is peculiarly apt.

66 *That ol' boy's a great rambler* — that poor old man talks a great deal of nonsense (dialect).

66 *Tent decent* — it's not decent (dialect).

67 *Let en be* — leave him alone (dialect).

67 *Let en bear his cross in peace* — let him endure his personal sufferings without interference. A New Testament reference.

Act III

Scene One

68 *all in* — exhausted (colloquial).

68 *off the road* — straying from the proper route.

69 *a deserter* — a soldier who has run away from his military duties. During active fighting this is considered a very serious offence, usually punishable by death; assisting a deserter can bring severe penalties.

69 *under the lady's feet* — in the lady's way, a distracting nuisance.

70 *one a the best* — one of the most trustworthy and humane men in the world (colloquial).

70 *very well fixed* — have arranged your life very comfortably (colloquial).

70 *yer must be hard pressed* — you must be under considerable strain, having to work very hard. The deserter assumes this since there seem to be so few people to do the necessary work.

70 *a fair bit a* — a good deal of, a lot of (dialect).

70 *a batman* — a soldier acting as personal servant to an officer.

70 *your class a person* — somebody of your status and quality.

71 *men of the world* — men of wide experience.

71 *thugs* — brutally violent men, usually of little intelligence but physically strong.

71 *couldn't 'urt a fly* — would be incapable of causing pain to anyone at all.

71 *a punishment squad* — a group of men being given particularly arduous and unpleasant work as a punishment for some offence.

71 *the black market* — illegal trading in goods banned by the state, or in short supply, or so as to avoid paying taxes.

71 *bin off me 'ead* — been mad, out of my mind (dialect).

71 *Thass 'ow we 'eard a you* — that's how we heard about you.

71 *an' they give yer up?* — and they told the authorities about you, *or* and they stopped being interested in you.

72 *he'll turn up* — he will suddenly appear.

73 *we're for it* — we'll be in serious trouble.

73 *floggin' snout t' cons* — selling tobacco to the prisoners (dialect).

74 *mess you about* — treat you badly, take advantage of you.

74 *We 'ave t' act fly* — we must cautiously and cunningly (dialect).

Scene Two

75 *infiltrate the camps* — get our supporters into the army and prisoner camps secretly, to win people over to our cause.

76 *give myself up* — voluntarily return to the military authorities for punishment.

76 *a passion* — an intensely felt commitment. 'Passion' also has the sense of noble suffering for a cause, such as the Passion of Christ.

77 *harbouring* — giving shelter and protection to.

77 *with retrospective effect* — the law will be applied to actions committed at a time before the new law made them illegal.

77 *dealing on the unauthorized market* — selling goods illegally. (See note on p. 71.)

77 *mandatory* — must be carried out, cannot be softened.

77 *a social liability* — a danger to other people, a bad influence.

77 *on me records* — written on my police or government documents.

78 *vetted* — checked, examined.

78 *a little swindler* — an unimportant, not particularly successful cheat, trickster.

79 *flailing* — hitting out wildly.

80 *backing out* — giving up, retreating.

80 *livid* — glaring and unhealthy looking.

82 *gropes* — searches about clumsily and blindly.

82 *owl* — a bird traditionally associated with death.

82 *fox* — an animal thought to be adept at survival because cunning.

84 *might would always be right* — this is a familiar saying, generally used to mean that those who were powerful would feel justified in doing whatever they wished for no better reason than that they had the power to do so. The weak and the helpless would have no rights. However, Bond has explained it differently:

> I think this means that if a god had really made the world he wouldn't have included in it evil and so there would be no weak and helpless at the mercy of the predatious. In other words, the weak and helpless would automatically have rights, or rather (since this would be paradise) they wouldn't have to claim rights in what would automatically be given to them anyway.

87 *my breath's short* — I become breathless very quickly.

87 *got no edge* — is no longer sharp.

87 *boy* — the farmer's son uses this as a term of familiarity, despite Lear's age.

88 *make my mark* — do something to be remembered by, be effective in some way.

88 *pick en up* — take the body away.

88 *shepherds* — urges them off, as if he were driving sheep.

Above: Lear and Cordelia under threat (end Act 1 Scene 7). Royal Court, 1971. *Below:* Fontanelle, Gravedigger's Boy and Lear (Act 2 Scene 6). RSC, 1982.

Above: Fontanelle, North, Cornwall and Bodice (Act 1 Scene 3).
Below: Fontanelle, Warrington and Soldier A (Act 1 Scene 4).
Opposite: Lear and his daughters. RSC, 1982.

Lear and Gravedigger's Boy. *Above:* Act 1 Scene 6; *below:* middle of Act 2 Scene 6; *opposite:* end of Act 2 Scene 6. RSC, 1982.

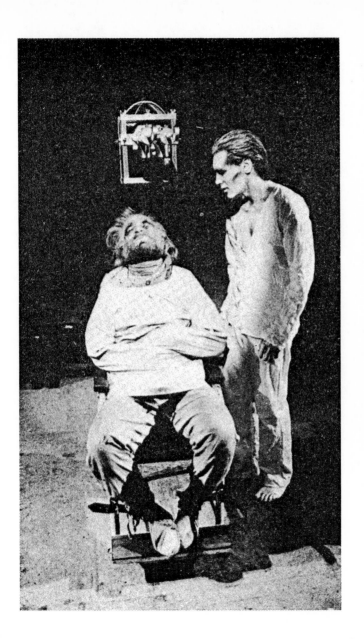

Above: Cordelia (Act 1 Scene 7). *Below:* Lear, Gravedigger's Boy, Carpenter and Cordelia (Act 3 Scene 3). RSC, 1982.

Appendix

For this new edition there follows an updated list of the first performances of Edward Bond's plays:

Play	First performance
The Pope's Wedding	9.12.1962
Saved	3.11.1965
A Chaste Maid in Cheapside (*adaptation*)	13.1.1966
The Three Sisters (*translation*)	18.4.1967
Early Morning	31.3.1968
Narrow Road to the Deep North	24.6.1968
Black Mass (*part of* Sharpeville Sequence)	22.3.1970
Passion	11.4.1971
Lear	29.9.1971
The Sea	22.5.1973
Bingo: Scenes of money and death	14.11.1973
Spring Awakening (*translation*)	28.5.1974
The Fool: Scenes of bread and love	18.11.1975
Stone	8.6.1976
We Come to the River (*music* H. W. Henze)	12.7.1976
The White Devil (*adaptation*)	12.7.1976
Grandma Faust (*part one of* A-A-America!)	25.10.1976
The Swing (*part two of* A-A-America!)	22.11.1976
The Bundle: New Narrow Road to the Deep North	13.1.1978
The Woman	10.8.1978
The Worlds	8.3.1979
Restoration	21.7.1981
Orpheus (*music* H. W. Henze)	2.11.1981
Summer	27.1.1982
Derek	18.10.1982
After the Assassinations	1.3.1983
The Cat (*music* H. W. Henze)	2.6.1983
Human Cannon	2.2.1986
The War Plays	
Part I: Red Black and Ignorant	29.5.1985

Questions for further study

1 Discuss the importance of the theme of justice in *Lear*.
2 How are family and personal relationships treated in *Lear* and what bearing do they have on the play's main themes?
3 Consider the dramatic handling of literal and metaphorical notions of vision and blindness in *Lear*.
4 Comment on the ways in which the imagery of imprisonment is deployed in *Lear*.
5 'Act One shows a world dominated by myth. Act Two shows the clash between myth and reality [. . .]. Act Three shows a resolution of this, in the world we prove real by dying in it.' In what ways does Bond's statement assist a discussion of the meaning of *Lear*?
6 To what ends and to what effect does Bond deploy the idea of 'the ghost' in *Lear*?
7 'An unwittingly presumptuous distillation of the naive, the banal and the portentous', or 'a powerful stage metaphor reminiscent of the Jacobean dramatists'? How would *you* describe Bond's *Lear* and why?
8 How convincingly does *Lear* (taking a leaf out of Shakespeare's *King Lear*) deal with concepts of nature and the unnatural?
9 In his preface to *Lear* Edward Bond expresses his hostility to the notion of 'socialised morality'. In what ways does the play make this explicit?
10 Bond insists that *Lear* is an optimistic play. Give grounds for agreeing or disagreeing with his view.
11 What is the dramatic function of food and drink in *Lear*?
12 The cast list calls for as many as fifteen soldiers who are differentiated alphabetically from A to O. What point do you think is being made and in what ways, if any, does the play manage to justify the apparent necessity for this number of 'extras'?
13 'A propaganda play must be able to tell its message to an uninformed or resisting audience' (Edward Bond). Is *Lear* a propaganda play and, if so, are propaganda and art in this instance at odds with one another?
14 The Greek theatre reported scenes of violence which occurred

offstage, while the Elizabethan theatre tended to show them onstage but in an overtly theatrical context. Does the literal, even naturalistic, representation of violence in Bond's *Lear* work and is it dramatically justified? (You might like to compare Lear's blinding in Bond with the blinding of Gloucester in Shakespeare's play.)

15 How effectively and to what ends does Bond deploy the various linguistic registers (ranging from the poetic to the crudely vernacular) in *Lear*?

16 How vital are the stage directions in *Lear*?

17 Scenes of violence and mayhem in *Lear* tend to be accompanied by language which is offhand, blasé, low key or even comic. What is the point of this strategy and how do you respond to it?

18 Bond's *Lear* has been described as a mixture of the naturalistic, the symbolic and the expressionistic. To what elements of the play do you think these descriptions refer and to what extent do you think they cohere dramatically?

19 'The only notable thing about Bond's *Lear* is the prestige it gains through vicarious association with Shakespeare's play.' Does Bond's play suffer from comparison with Shakespeare or would its merits still be apparent if it was called something different and Cordelia and the Duke of Cornwall renamed?

20 '*Lear* seems to advocate social revolution but is critical of those who mistakenly replace one form of tyranny with another.' Discuss.

Methuen Drama Student Editions

Jean Anouilh *Antigone* • John Arden *Serjeant Musgrave's Dance*
Alan Ayckbourn *Confusions* • Aphra Behn *The Rover* • Edward Bond
Lear • *Saved* • Bertolt Brecht *The Caucasian Chalk Circle* • *Fear and
Misery in the Third Reich* • *The Good Person of Szechwan* • *Life of Galileo* •
Mother Courage and her Children • *The Resistible Rise of Arturo Ui* • *The
Threepenny Opera* • Anton Chekhov *The Cherry Orchard* • *The Seagull* •
Three Sisters • *Uncle Vanya* • Caryl Churchill *Serious Money* • *Top Girls*
• Shelagh Delaney *A Taste of Honey* • Euripides Elektra • *Medea*•
Dario Fo *Accidental Death of an Anarchist* • Michael Frayn *Copenhagen*
• John Galsworthy *Strife* • Nikolai Gogol *The Government Inspector* •
Robert Holman *Across Oka* • Henrik Ibsen *A Doll's House* • *Ghosts*•
Hedda Gabler • Charlotte Keatley *My Mother Said I Never Should* •
Bernard Kops *Dreams of Anne Frank* • Federico García Lorca *Blood
Wedding* • *Doña Rosita the Spinster* (bilingual edition) • *The House of
Bernarda Alba* • (bilingual edition) • *Yerma* (bilingual edition) • David
Mamet *Glengarry Glen Ross* • *Oleanna* • Patrick Marber *Closer* • John
Marston *The Malcontent* • Martin McDonagh *The Lieutenant of Inishmore* •
Joe Orton *Loot* • Luigi Pirandello *Six Characters in Search of an Author*
• Mark Ravenhill *Shopping and F***ing* • Willy Russell *Blood Brothers*
• *Educating Rita* • Sophocles *Antigone* • *Oedipus the King* • Wole
Soyinka *Death and the King's Horseman* • Shelagh Stephenson *The
Memory of Water* • August Strindberg *Miss Julie* • J. M. Synge *The
Playboy of the Western World* • Theatre Workshop *Oh What a Lovely
War* Timberlake Wertenbaker *Our Country's Good* • Arnold Wesker
The Merchant • Oscar Wilde *The Importance of Being Earnest* •
Tennessee Williams *A Streetcar Named Desire* • *The Glass Menagerie*

Methuen Drama Modern Plays

include work by

Edward Albee
Jean Anouilh
John Arden
Margaretta D'Arcy
Peter Barnes
Sebastian Barry
Brendan Behan
Dermot Bolger
Edward Bond
Bertolt Brecht
Howard Brenton
Anthony Burgess
Simon Burke
Jim Cartwright
Caryl Churchill
Complicite
Noël Coward
Lucinda Coxon
Sarah Daniels
Nick Darke
Nick Dear
Shelagh Delaney
David Edgar
David Eldridge
Dario Fo
Michael Frayn
John Godber
Paul Godfrey
David Greig
John Guare
Peter Handke
David Harrower
Jonathan Harvey
Iain Heggie
Declan Hughes
Terry Johnson
Sarah Kane
Charlotte Keatley
Barrie Keeffe

Howard Korder
Robert Lepage
Doug Lucie
Martin McDonagh
John McGrath
Terrence McNally
David Mamet
Patrick Marber
Arthur Miller
Mtwa, Ngema & Simon
Tom Murphy
Phyllis Nagy
Peter Nichols
Sean O'Brien
Joseph O'Connor
Joe Orton
Louise Page
Joe Penhall
Luigi Pirandello
Stephen Poliakoff
Franca Rame
Mark Ravenhill
Philip Ridley
Reginald Rose
Willy Russell
Jean-Paul Sartre
Sam Shepard
Wole Soyinka
Simon Stephens
Shelagh Stephenson
Peter Straughan
C. P. Taylor
Theatre Workshop
Sue Townsend
Judy Upton
Timberlake Wertenbaker
Roy Williams
Snoo Wilson
Victoria Wood

Methuen Drama Contemporary Dramatists
include

John Arden (two volumes)
Arden & D'Arcy
Peter Barnes (three volumes)
Sebastian Barry
Dermot Bolger
Edward Bond (eight volumes)
Howard Brenton
  (two volumes)
Richard Cameron
Jim Cartwright
Caryl Churchill (two volumes)
Sarah Daniels (two volumes)
Nick Darke
David Edgar (three volumes)
David Eldridge
Ben Elton
Dario Fo (two volumes)
Michael Frayn (three volumes)
David Greig
John Godber (four volumes)
Paul Godfrey
John Guare
Lee Hall (two volumes)
Peter Handke
Jonathan Harvey
  (two volumes)
Declan Hughes
Terry Johnson (three volumes)
Sarah Kane
Barrie Keeffe
Bernard-Marie Koltès
  (two volumes)
Franz Xaver Kroetz
David Lan
Bryony Lavery
Deborah Levy
Doug Lucie

David Mamet (four volumes)
Martin McDonagh
Duncan McLean
Anthony Minghella
  (two volumes)
Tom Murphy (six volumes)
Phyllis Nagy
Anthony Neilsen (two volumes)
Philip Osment
Gary Owen
Louise Page
Stewart Parker (two volumes)
Joe Penhall (two volumes)
Stephen Poliakoff
  (three volumes)
David Rabe (two volumes)
Mark Ravenhill (two volumes)
Christina Reid
Philip Ridley
Willy Russell
Eric-Emmanuel Schmitt
Ntozake Shange
Sam Shepard (two volumes)
Wole Soyinka (two volumes)
Simon Stephens (two volumes)
Shelagh Stephenson
David Storey (three volumes)
Sue Townsend
Judy Upton
Michel Vinaver
  (two volumes)
Arnold Wesker (two volumes)
Michael Wilcox
Roy Williams (three volumes)
Snoo Wilson (two volumes)
David Wood (two volumes)
Victoria Wood

Methuen Drama World Classics

include

Jean Anouilh (two volumes)
Brendan Behan
Aphra Behn
Bertolt Brecht (eight volumes)
Büchner
Bulgakov
Calderón
Čapek
Anton Chekhov
Noël Coward (eight volumes)
Feydeau (two volumes)
Eduardo De Filippo
Max Frisch
John Galsworthy
Gogol
Gorky (two volumes)
Harley Granville Barker
(two volumes)
Victor Hugo
Henrik Ibsen (six volumes)
Jarry

Lorca (three volumes)
Marivaux
Mustapha Matura
David Mercer (two volumes)
Arthur Miller (six volumes)
Molière
Musset
Peter Nichols (two volumes)
Joe Orton
A. W. Pinero
Luigi Pirandello
Terence Rattigan
(two volumes)
W. Somerset Maugham
(two volumes)
August Strindberg
(three volumes)
J. M. Synge
Ramón del Valle-Inclán
Frank Wedekind
Oscar Wilde

Methuen Drama Classical Greek Dramatists

Aeschylus Plays: One
(Persians, Seven Against Thebes, Suppliants,
Prometheus Bound)

Aeschylus Plays: Two
(Oresteia: Agamemnon, Libation-Bearers, Eumenides)

Aristophanes Plays: One
(Acharnians, Knights, Peace, Lysistrata)

Aristophanes Plays: Two
(Wasps, Clouds, Birds, Festival Time, Frogs)

Aristophanes & Menander: New Comedy
(Women in Power, Wealth, The Malcontent,
The Woman from Samos)

Euripides Plays: One
(Medea, The Phoenician Women, Bacchae)

Euripides Plays: Two
(Hecuba, The Women of Troy, Iphigeneia at Aulis,
Cyclops)

Euripides Plays: Three
(Alkestis, Helen, Ion)

Euripides Plays: Four
(Elektra, Orestes, Iphigeneia in Tauris)

Euripides Plays: Five
(Andromache, Herakles' Children, Herakles)

Euripides Plays: Six
(Hippolytos, Suppliants, Rhesos)

Sophocles Plays: One
(Oedipus the King, Oedipus at Colonus, Antigone)

Sophocles Plays: Two
(Ajax, Women of Trachis, Electra, Philoctetes)

For a complete catalogue of Methuen Drama titles
write to:

Methuen Drama
50 Bedford Square
London
WC1B 3DP

or you can visit our website at:

www.methuendrama.com